THE FORGETTABLES

The
FORGETTABLES

REMARKABLE IRISH PEOPLE (AND ANIMALS) YOU'VE NEVER HEARD OF

MYLES DUNGAN

ILLUSTRATED BY ALAN DUNNE

GILL BOOKS

Gill Books
Hume Avenue
Park West
Dublin 12
www.gillbooks.ie

Gill Books is an imprint of M.H. Gill and Co.

Text © Myles Dungan 2023
Illustrations © Alan Dunne 2023

978 07171 99143

Designed by Graham Thew
Edited by Michelle Griffin
Proofread by Emma Dunne
Printed and bound by Hussar Books, Poland
This book is typeset in 11pt English Grotesque.

The paper used in this book comes from the wood pulp of sustainably
managed forests.

A CIP catalogue record for this book is available from the British Library.

5 4 3 2 1

For Ollie, Sadie, Sophie, Ben, Noah and Leo

Myles

For Gráinne, Tadhg, Louise, Emma, Paul, Nuala and John

Alan

CONTENTS

INTRODUCTION

This is a book about some really extraordinary and interesting Irish men, women and even animals. No, I'm not talking about Mary Robinson, Brian O'Driscoll, Katie McCabe, Roy Keane, Rhasidat Adeleke, W.B. Yeats, Nijinsky or Seamus Heaney. You've probably heard of all of them. They've won Nobel Prizes, Premier League titles, elections, an Epsom Derby and broken a host of Irish sprint records, so they're all rather famous.

That's the point of *The Forgettables*: I want to introduce you to some fascinating Irish pioneers that you're very unlikely to have heard of, and that's all right, because almost no one has. They were outstanding in their own fields – it's just that sometimes the field in question, while important, was a bit obscure. Unless you have an interest in submarines you probably won't have heard of John Holland, the Clareman who invented them. If you're into astronomy you might have heard of the Earl of Rosse, who built what was once the biggest telescope in the world. Otherwise, probably not.

Mostly what our trailblazers achieved, discovered, bought, sold or dreamed up was perfectly legal. Mostly. But not always. I certainly wouldn't want to encourage anyone to do things that are against the law (this book contains lots of warnings against trying out some of the things you'll be reading about), but I have to admit that some of our dodgier pioneers ('Underrated Rogues') are every bit as captivating (and often more fun) than the more clever and upstanding exhibits in this museum of Irish achievement. While we always want the good guy to win in the movie, it wouldn't be nearly as interesting without the bad guy.

So, buckle up and get ready to meet the man who discovered why the sky is blue; the inventor of the potato crisp; one of the bravest pigeons in the history of feathered flight; one of the nastiest landlords in the history of rent; one of the worst bishops in the history of religion; and one of the worst poets in the history of rhyme.

P.S. One of our featured players is utterly and entirely fictional; they did not exist – I just made them up for the craic. See if you can figure out which of them is simply the most unbelievable. The answer is at the back. Don't peek now!

P.P.S. You will have to endure some really lousy dad jokes along the way. Feel free to groan loudly.

PART I

NEGLECTED NOBLES

Ireland has always had noblemen and noblewomen. In the dim and distant past they were High Kings and Queens, or clan chieftains who would be honoured by being called 'The'. An odd sort of title, you might think, except that, for example, the head of the O'Rahilly clan would be called 'The O'Rahilly' (he still is, as a matter of fact!).

After the Normans arrived in Ireland in the 12th century, the ancient Gaelic titles existed for a while alongside those of the invaders, before they slowly began to disappear. Gaelic chieftains were replaced by British lords, ladies, earls, dukes and duchesses. As the land of Ireland changed hands, the ancient Irish nobility was replaced by a new Anglo-Irish aristocracy (landowners). Not all of them had titles; some were just plain 'Mr' or 'Mrs', like Richard 'Humanity Dick' Martin, who campaigned for years against cruelty to animals.

Some members of the Irish nobility were not especially 'noble', by the way. They didn't all use their power and wealth for good purposes.

Time to meet some of the most interesting Irish aristocrats: people who pretty much did as they liked, and usually got away with it.

QUEEN GORMLAITH

She married a number of powerful men
and outlived the lot of them.

ONE OF THE FUN things about a lot of figures in ancient Irish history is in trying to separate facts from legends. A lot of the information we have about High Kings, rebellious wives, warring chieftains, druids, magic potions and a salmon which, when boiled and eaten with a nice garnish bestowed amazing knowledge, wasn't written down until centuries after they were all dead. Where did the historians of the 10th, 11th and 12th centuries get their information about people who had lived hundreds of years before? Mostly from word of mouth. They would take the stories they had picked up from local folklore and write them down. Or sometimes they just ripped off the work of earlier historians, who had also got their information from popular legends. And please don't say this too loudly or you will give historians a bad name, but sometimes they might even have made some stuff up!

Take Queen Gormlaith, for example. First things first, at least we know that she did exist. She was Gormlaith Ní Murchada, daughter of the King of Leinster. Her first husband was the Viking ruler of Dublin Olaf Cuaran, whom she married sometime before 981. We know that's true because Olaf died at the Battle of Tara in 981, so he would not have been available for weddings and honeymoons after that date. Gormlaith might (or might not) have then married Máel Sechnaill Mac Domnaill, King of Meath and High King of Ireland, the warrior chieftain who defeated Olaf at Tara. This might (or might not) have been because he won her in the battle, or it was just his way of showing there were no hard feelings that he had made her a widow.

Or was it because she wanted to get close enough to kill him and gain revenge? Some accounts say that, while she was extremely beautiful and charming, she was also toxic. Pure evil.

We know that she (probably) married another Irish High King, Brian Boru, in 999. He had replaced Máel Sechnaill as High King, and clearly Gormlaith had a thing for High Kings, so she must have ditched Máel Sechnaill in favour of Brian. After that it all gets a bit murky – as if it wasn't already murky enough! There are rumours that she divorced Brian and spent the rest of her life trying to get her own back on her ex.

There are other stories that she and Brian remained (unhappily) married but that she tried to get her brother to kill the High King instead of just divorcing him. Divorce was a lot simpler in 11th century Ireland but having someone murdered was dead simple. Literally.

The other thing we can be pretty certain about is that she outlived Brian (her husband, or her ex-husband) by 16 years, dying in 1030.

Glad we could clear all of that up. Still confused? Sorry, you're on your own. There is only so much a modern scribe can do.

PHOTO

NAME GORMLAITH NÍ MURCHADA
(960-1030)

OCCUPATION BEING A QUEEN

WHAT WE KNOW ABOUT HER:	Not a whole lot
LIKES:	Starting wars (maybe, maybe not)
DISLIKES:	Brian Boru (maybe, maybe not)
CLAIM TO FAME:	Brian Boru (maybe, maybe not)

MARGARET O'CARROLL

She was the medieval 'hostess with the mostest' and a courageous pilgrim.

WHAT DO YOU do when you're married to a king who likes to conquer his neighbour's territory or steal his cattle before he sits down to breakfast? If it's the 15th century, if you're living in the Irish midlands and if you're Margaret O'Carroll, you try to compensate for such bad behaviour by doing lots and lots of good works, in the hope that God and the king of England are so distracted by what a generous soul you are that they don't take it out on your husband.

When I say that Margaret's husband, Calvach O'Connor, was a king, that is probably pushing it. He wasn't king of very much, just modern-day Offaly in the Irish midlands and one or two fields beyond that. But he seems to have spent most of his adult life raiding, pillaging and fighting, so his wife

felt the need to compensate for hubby's very obvious and lethal personality flaws.

Known to one and all as 'Margaret the Hospitable', instead of kidnapping, stealing or beheading people, Margaret O'Carroll, Queen of Offaly, made lots of charitable donations to the poor and was a huge patron of the arts. In between having seven children and trying to be supportive of her warlike husband as he chewed up his neighbours, in 1433 she threw two enormous parties. These were festivals to which poets, musicians and the poor (often one and the same thing) were invited. Almost 3,000 people attended the first feast in March while Margaret, dressed in a magnificent coat of 'cloth of gold' (it's exactly what it sounds like), watched them from the battlements of her castle. In case anyone tried to steal the spoons,

Calvach roamed among the tables, keeping manners on the guests. There were no reports of any trouble whatsoever. Why do you think that was?

Margaret was a very religious woman, and in 1445 decided to join a number of other Gaelic nobles on a pilgrimage to the shrine of St James of Compostela in Spain. That was not as easy as it might sound: there were no Ryanair flights to Compostela, or even Bilbao, the nearest large city; you could easily drown on your way there or back (one of the pilgrims did); and if you managed to escape a watery grave, you might be captured by pirates and held to ransom. Unlike a number of her fellow pilgrims (three of whom died), Margaret survived the experience and made her way back to the arms (as in limbs, not swords or lances for once) of Calvach, who was so pleased to see her that he took a couple of days off invading and killing his neighbours to celebrate her return.

In 1451, Margaret sadly passed away, dying either of cancer or leprosy, which was quite common in medieval Ireland. The historians of her day (known as 'annalists') described her as 'the best woman of the Gael'.

She certainly knew how to throw a party.

PHOTO

NAME MARGARET O'CARROLL
(C. 1400-1451)

OCCUPATION ANOTHER QUEEN

LIKELY TO SAY:	'Ah, go on, go on. Have some more venison. Ye will, ye will.'
LIKES:	Dispensing charity
DISLIKES:	Sore feet
CLAIM TO FAME:	Throwing feasts, making a pilgrimage to Compostela

LORD BELVEDERE

Nobody told him about 'brotherly love',
so he didn't bother with it.

IN THE ORNATE and splendid grounds of Belvedere House outside Mullingar you can see the ruins of what looks like an old monastery or church, the shell of a bygone age.

Except that's not what it is at all. It's a shell all right, but that's actually how it was built. The so-called 'Jealous Wall' was erected by Robert Rochfort, 1st Earl of Belvedere ('earl' is the next step up from 'lord' and 'viscount') and is what is known as a 'folly'. These were apparently useless structures built (usually in the 1700s) by wealthy aristocrats in order to impress the neighbours. (Another example is the Spire of Lloyd outside Kells, County Meath, built by the Earl of Bective. Although it is 80 kilometres inland, the Spire of Lloyd looks exactly like a coastal lighthouse.) Why did these rich aristocrats build follies? Because they could.

Robert's folly is the biggest in the country. The Jealous Wall, however, had another function. It blocked his view of his brother George Rochfort's magnificent home, Tudenham House, a few kilometres away. Robert, you see, didn't get on with his brothers. He certainly didn't want to be reminded that George had built a better-looking house than his own.

George got off lightly. His other brother, Arthur, did not. In 1736, Robert married the 16-year-old Mary Molesworth. After a few years of marriage, he accused her, out of the blue, of having an affair with Arthur.

Robert sued Arthur and won what was then a huge award of £2,000 (that's around €500,000 today). Arthur couldn't pay and fled the country. A few years later Arthur was assured by his brother that all was forgiven. He returned to Ireland and was immediately thrown in jail by the treacherous Robert, where, after a few years, he died.

Mary, Robert's young wife, was even less fortunate. She was imprisoned by her evil husband in the couple's home for more than 30 years. She managed to escape just once and fled to her family in Dublin. Robert came after her, reclaimed what he believed to be his 'property' (women had almost no rights in the 18th century) and returned her to captivity. Only when he died (he was

mysteriously beaten to death – probably by some of his tenants, who had no great love for him) was she released by their son. By then she had lost her reason and used to wander around the house talking to the portraits. She died shortly after regaining her freedom.

Robert could just as easily have slotted into our 'Underrated Rogues' section!

Today Belvedere House and its gardens are beautifully preserved by Westmeath County Council while the nearby Tudenham House, once a far more spectacular building, lies in ruins. The revolting Robert Rochfort, 1st Earl of Belvedere, would be pleased.

PHOTO

NAME ROBERT ROCHFORT, 1ST EARL OF BELVEDERE (1708-1774)

OCCUPATION(S) POLITICIAN, LANDLORD, LOUSY HUSBAND

UNLIKELY TO SAY:	'He ain't heavy, he's my brother'
LIKES:	Control
DISLIKES:	His brothers, his wife … people in general
CLAIM TO FAME:	Imprisoning his wife, suing his brother, building the Jealous Wall

GEORGE ROBERT FITZGERALD

He liked hanging out with bears
and kidnapped his own father.

POOR COUNTY MAYO often drew the short straw when it came to the oddballs who owned land there in the 1700s and 1800s. They didn't come any odder and meaner than George Robert Fitzgerald, known to his friends and enemies as 'Fighting' Fitzgerald because of the number of times he faced other noblemen with a pistol or sword in his hand while taking part in one of the favourite hobbies of the well-off in 18th century Ireland, killing each other in duels. Ireland was famous for the level of duelling among the members of the upper classes. As there was no Google around to settle arguments, it was easier to challenge someone you disagreed with to a duel – and kill him.

George counts as a nobleman by virtue of the vast amount of land he owned. His eccentricity might have had something to do with a blow he received to his head when he was in his twenties.

George was the nephew of a bishop, but that was about as close as he ever got to goodness. Like a lot of his fellow aristocrats (his 'peers'), he liked to drink, to gamble and to shoot people who annoyed him. One of his claims to fame was that he was kicked out of a gambling den in Paris by the king of France himself! He would have liked nothing better than to dispose of King Charles X in single combat, but you weren't allowed to challenge French (or English) kings to a duel.

Otherwise, we'd probably be up to King Charles XIII of England by now.

Altogether, George probably fought at least 30 men. He must have been good because, according to the law of averages, he would never have survived that many duels if he hadn't been a deadly shot. He was also lucky not to have been murdered by one of his tenants. Those he would terrorise while out hunting by torchlight. He took his pet bears along as bodyguards. Come to think of it, he was probably more fortunate the bears didn't get him before the tenants.

George once took the unusual step of kidnapping his own father (please don't try this at home) with whom he was constantly at loggerheads over money. He imprisoned his dad on an island in Clew Bay. This may not sound like a very nice way to treat one's old man, but it gets worse … after a while, George chained his dad to a bear!

George came to a bad end. When a solicitor with whom he was feuding was murdered, George was suspected of having done away with the man. He was put on trial and found guilty of killing his enemy. He was hanged in Castlebar in 1786. Although they could probably have intervened, the bears decided to let the law take its course. Even they must have been fed up with George by then.

PHOTO

NAME GEORGE ROBERT 'FIGHTING' FITZGERALD (1748–1786)

OCCUPATION(S) LANDOWNER, GAMBLER, DUELLIST

UNLIKELY TO SAY:	'Hey, Dad, let's go for a pizza.'
LIKES:	Bears
DISLIKES:	His father
CLAIM TO FAME:	Terrorised County Mayo and abducted his father

RICHARD MARTIN

The early-19th-century campaigner against cruelty to animals.

IN THE 18TH and 19th centuries, most Irish peasant farmers did not have an easy time. They were tenants of wealthy landowners, which meant they didn't own their own farms but paid rent twice a year to their landlords. Many of them had farms that were tiny by today's standards. Some were smaller than five acres in size and could only support a family because of how easy it was to grow potatoes, the staple diet of more than a third of the Irish people. However, bad and all as things were for peasant farmers, they were even worse for their animals.

Just take one example. When there was a dispute between farmers, or between tenants and their landlord, it was far easier to take out your anger on your enemy's animals than on your enemy himself. This gave rise to a cruel practice called 'houghing', where the legs of cattle would be sliced with a knife, making the poor animals lame. In addition, some of the so-called 'sports' in Ireland and Britain at that time were particularly cruel: like dog fighting, or cock fighting, or bear baiting (in which a chained bear was forced to fight a pack of dogs). All of these attracted a lot of money in betting.

One man who devoted much of his life to improving the lot of animals was the landowner and politician Richard Martin from Galway. He spoke out in the British parliament against the ill-treatment of animals and was often laughed and jeered at. But it was through his efforts that a law was passed in 1822 making it illegal for farmers to ill-treat cattle. In 1824 he became one of the founders of the Society for the Prevention of Cruelty to Animals.

However, 'Humanity Dick' (King George IV gave him the nickname) was not as tolerant towards his fellow human beings as he was towards animals. Over his lifetime he is said to have fought over one hundred duels – his other nickname, not nearly so complimentary, was 'Hairtrigger Dick'. One of the men he killed in a duel was his own cousin.

Neither was he very good at paying his debts. He managed to keep his creditors (people to whom he owed money) at bay when he was a member of parliament, but when he lost his seat in the House of Commons in 1826, he had to flee to France, where he died in 1834.

So, a bit of a mixed bag was Richard Martin. He did a lot of good as Humanity Dick, caused much havoc and injury with his pistols as Hairtrigger Dick, and angered a lot of people to whom he owed a small fortune as 'Gimme the Money, Dick'. (OK, so I made that last one up!)

PHOTO

NAME RICHARD MARTIN (1754–1834)

OCCUPATION(S) LANDOWNER, POLITICIAN, CAMPAIGNER

NICKNAMES:	'Humanity Dick'/'Hairtrigger Dick'
LIKES:	Animals
DISLIKES:	People who harmed animals, creditors
CLAIM TO FAME:	A campaigner against cruelty to animals, and one of the founders, in 1824, of the Society for the Prevention of Cruelty to Animals

THE 3RD EARL OF LUCAN

The man who lost the famous Light Brigade at the Battle of Balaclava.

THERE IS OFTEN a very good reason why Irish noblemen are 'neglected'. It's because they richly deserve to be. None more so than George Charles Bingham, 3rd Earl of Lucan, a nasty piece of work who inherited 60,000 acres of land in Mayo and spent much of the Great Famine getting rid of his tenants. He's the sort of person you would be expected to boo and hiss if he turned up in a Christmas panto. He went to a posh private school in England and joined the British Army at the age of 16. Worse luck for the army, as it turned out!

Between 1853 and 1856, Britain fought an ugly war against Russia in Crimea. George was the man in charge of the British Army's horse soldiers, the cavalry. Under his command was his brother-in-law, Lord Cardigan, who led a cavalry unit called the Light Brigade. There was no brotherly-in-law love between these two. They hated each other with a passion and were not even on speaking terms. At the Battle of Balaclava in 1854, George ordered Cardigan and the Light Brigade to charge the Russian artillery, a collection of huge cannons. That's like sending a gazelle to attack a lion. The result was entirely predictable: the Light Brigade was slaughtered by Russian cannon balls. George was sacked and brought back to England.

The great poet Alfred, Lord Tennyson wrote a famous poem 'The Charge of the Light Brigade',

which included the line 'Into the valley of Death rode the six hundred'. Well, they weren't there by accident. They had been sent to their doom by George.

Of course, in those days, as long as you were an aristocrat, you usually just got a slap on the wrist for causing the deaths of hundreds of men. So George was able to spend the next few years sulking on his estate in Mayo.

But George's return to Ireland was not good news for his tenants. They had been praying that he would fall victim to a Russian bullet, or a fatal disease. This was because of his reign of terror during the Great Famine of the 1840s. When the potato crop failed hundreds of thousands of Irish farmers couldn't afford to pay rent to their landlords. Many landlords were patient and treated their tenants well. George was not one of those. He began to throw hundreds of his tenants out on the side of the road, making paupers of them. When they responded by burning an effigy (a dummy) of George in Castlebar, he rode into their midst, sword flashing, shouting, 'I'll evict the lot of ye.' He was as good as his word. He didn't like Catholics either and once said his reason for evicting so many tenants was that he would 'not breed paupers to pay priests'. His starving tenants were replaced by herds of sheep and cattle. Long may we continue to 'neglect' Lord Lucan.

PHOTO

NAME GEORGE CHARLES BINGHAM, 3RD EARL OF LUCAN (1800-1888)

OCCUPATION(S) SOLDIER, LANDLORD

UNLIKELY TO SAY:	'Into the valley of Death rode the six hundred.'
LIKES:	Evicting tenants
DISLIKES:	Balaclavas, the poetry of Alfred, Lord Tennyson
CLAIM TO FAME:	Evicted hundreds during the Great Famine and sent the Light Brigade to its doom at the Battle of Balaclava)

ELLEN CUFFE

Was she the most important Jewish woman in Irish history?

ELLEN BISCHOFFSHEIM WAS born in London, so obviously has no place in a book on exceptional (but un-celebrated) Irish people ... but Ellen Cuffe, a member of the Seanad, a campaigner for the revival of the Irish language, a woman who gave hundreds of thousands of pounds to Irish charities, and one of the most important Jewish women in Irish history, certainly has. The problem is that they are one and the same person. So, what's a guy to do? Leave her out? Not a chance.

Bischoffsheim was her maiden name and Ellen didn't get to Ireland until she married William Cuffe, the 4th Earl of Desart, in 1881. Marrying an earl made her a countess, but an Irish one. While living with her husband in Kilkenny, they got the idea to

build a village from scratch. That became Talbot's Inch on the outskirts of Kilkenny city. Sadly, the earl died less than 20 years after they married so they did not have that much time together. After Desart's death, Ellen might easily have decided to move back to England permanently, but she had become very interested in the Irish language and threw herself into a new cause. She wanted to hear more people speaking the language. She learned to speak Irish herself and joined the Gaelic League, the organisation set up in 1896 to revive Irish. Whenever she met people who claimed that Irish was a dead language and could never be revived, she would point to the success of Palestinian Jews in reviving Hebrew, a genuinely dead language that had not been spoken for centuries.

Because of her work for charity and for Gaelic she was appointed to the Senate of the newly independent Irish Free State in 1922. Although this was a very proper reward for all her work, it was also a bit ironic as she had been dead set against the idea of women getting the vote. Before the First World War, while the Suffragettes were campaigning for votes for women, Ellen was a leading light in an organisation called the National League for Opposing Women's Suffrage! That didn't make her very popular with early feminists. Neither did it stop her attending the Senate and speaking from time to time on issues that concerned her. She also took part in Senate votes! Perhaps she appreciated the irony, perhaps not.

When Ellen died, she left a large fortune (worth around €15 million today). This was distributed among a number of charities that she had supported during her lifetime.

PHOTO

NAME ELLEN ODETTE CUFFE
(NÉE BISCHOFFSHEIM),
COUNTESS OF DESART (1857-1933)

OCCUPATION(S) COUNTESSING
(OK, THERE'S NO SUCH WORD),
BEING A SENATOR

LIKELY TO SAY:	'Cad é mar atá tú?'
LIKES:	The Irish language, the Earl of Desart (her husband)
DISLIKES:	Votes for women
CLAIM TO FAME:	Gave millions to charities and fought to revive the Irish language

PART 2

HONOURABLE BUT UNDERAPPRECIATED

By now we've come across some ingenious, brave, talented, vicious, greedy Irish people. Time to meet a small, select group, who, in their own way, have made a difference to Ireland and/or the wider world by sticking to their principles, taking up causes that were unpopular or just doing their jobs.

Mary Harris from Cork is not well-known in her native country, but she became a beloved champion of underpaid and exploited American workers over a long lifetime. Georgina Frost is not a name that many people are familiar with, but she struck a huge blow in the 1920s for women who wanted to work. Valentine Greatrakes earned a reputation as a healer. Tony Small, Ted Sweeney and Maureen Sweeney just got on with things, but made their own mark in doing so.

It's high time they were honoured.

THE STROKER

VALENTINE GREATRAKES

He could heal people just by
touching them ... or could he?

WHENEVER MEDICAL scientists work on new drugs, at some point they need to try them out on real people to see if they work. They have to be careful of something called the 'placebo effect'. A placebo is a harmless pill that should have absolutely no impact whatever on a person's state of health. However, often when people are given a placebo they think they are being treated with a new miracle drug and start to get better, even if all they've been given is a mixture of flour and sugar dressed up as medication. It's all in the mind!

Was that what lay behind the story of Valentine Greatrakes, born in Waterford in 1628 and at one time a soldier in the army of Oliver Cromwell in the English Civil War? He's often been described as a 'faith healer' who had supposedly been given this gift to heal people just by touching them by God. Maybe he had been, or maybe his patients just thought he had, and they healed themselves ... the placebo effect strikes again.

While many people believed that Valentine was a healer, there were those who thought that he was an out-and-out 'quack': a charlatan (trickster) who preyed on the sick and convinced them (and perhaps even himself) that he was responsible for curing them of illnesses like fever, convulsions, gout and rheumatism by gently stroking them.

That is how he became known as 'The Stroker'. His short career as a healer began when he appeared to cure a boy from Lismore, County Waterford of a disease called scrofula (a nasty rash around the face and throat). When word got around, people began to flock to him and he had to set aside three days a week to treat them. That didn't last long, however, because he was ordered by the authorities to stop, as he did not have a licence to practise any form of medicine.

By then, news of his 'powers' had spread beyond Ireland and he was invited to come to England and work his miracle cures there. He became famous enough in England to be introduced to the king himself. Charles II was not convinced but, despite his scepticism, allowed Valentine to continue his work. Valentine then toured England and claimed to have cured many people of a number of ailments.

When he was attacked in a series of articles by English sceptics (disbelievers) Valentine gave up and returned to Ireland. There he lived quietly for the last 20 years of his life. At no point did he ever accept payment for his healing work, which surely means that whatever he might have been, he was certainly not a conman or a charlatan trying to profit from the misery of others.

PHOTO

NAME VALENTINE GREATRAKES, AKA 'THE STROKER' (1628-1683)

OCCUPATION(S) SOLDIER, FAITH HEALER

UNLIKELY TO SAY:	'That's a nasty wound there. I'd bring that to the doctor.'
LIKES:	The Bible
DISLIKES:	Disease
CLAIM TO FAME:	Travelled throughout Britain and Ireland curing people of a variety of diseases

TONY SMALL

He was impressively loyal to his employer,
and a rarity in 18th-century Dublin.

TONY SMALL WAS clever, loyal, resourceful and often heroic. He became close to one of the most famous and beloved noblemen, Lord Edward Fitzgerald, after saving his life. Although not born in Ireland he definitely qualifies as an honorary Irishman.

Imagine the scene. It is September 1781. A deadly battle has taken place between the two armies of the American War of Independence, in which America sought its independence from Britain. Hundreds of men are lying on the field of battle. Those left alive are being picked up by search parties and given help, but one young British Army officer has been overlooked by the rescuers. Unless Lord Edward Fitzgerald, son of the Duke of Leinster, is found and given assistance, he will certainly die of

his wounds. Wandering across the field, appalled by the death and destruction, is an escaped slave named Tony Small. Fortunately for Lord Edward, Tony finds him and he is able to recover from his wounds. In return for being rescued from the battlefield, Edward offers to employ Tony at a good salary and take him back to Ireland. There he would be safe from recapture as a runaway slave. It was the beginning of a relationship between two close friends, rather than between a man and his servant.

Until Edward's death as one of the leaders of rebellion of the United Irishmen in 1798, the two men were never apart. One of their first adventures together was an extraordinary trip down the Mississippi–Missouri river in a canoe; from close to the Canadian border they paddled all the way

south to New Orleans on the shores of the Gulf of Mexico. The journey took months and the two men were given up for dead.

Back in Dublin, Tony was an unusual sight. There were not many African Americans to be seen in the city in the 1780s. Lord Edward lived in Leinster House on Kildare Street, the building that is now Dáil Éireann. This was the magnificent home of his father, the Duke of Leinster. Tony would often be seen around the streets of Dublin running errands for his employer. He became well-known and popular. Edward thought so highly of Tony that he had the man's portrait painted by a professional artist. Tony repaid Edward's confidence and friendship on many occasions. Once, when Edward's enemies were searching for the Irish rebel leader, Tony managed to warn him (just in time) to flee from Leinster House. Sadly, he could not prevent his friend and employer from being betrayed by a British spy, and Edward was killed after a brief period spent in hiding, waiting for the rebellion of 1798 to begin.

After the death of Lord Edward, Tony moved to England with another of the Fitzgerald family servants. Little is known of his later married life in England, other than the fact that he set up a business in Piccadilly in the centre of London.

Small by name, but not by nature.

PHOTO

NAME TONY SMALL
(LATE-18TH CENTURY)

OCCUPATION(S) MANSERVANT,
BUSINESSMAN

TALENTS:	Being discreet, canoeing
LIKES:	Freedom
DISLIKES:	Slave owners
CLAIM TO FAME:	Companion of the great Irish rebel Lord Edward Fitzgerald

MARY 'MOTHER JONES' HARRIS

The 'grandmother of all agitators',
champion of the oppressed.

BECAUSE OF THE Great Famine (1845–50) Ireland lost a lot of good people through starvation, disease and emigration. One of those was Corkwoman Mary Harris, whose family left the country when she was a teenager in order to escape from the misery and poverty of the Famine years. But while she is almost unknown in Ireland, Mary is very famous indeed in her adopted home of the United States of America. She even has a magazine called after her, *Mother Jones,* the name by which she is celebrated in the USA.

How she came by that name is an interesting story. She married a man named Jones in Memphis, Tennessee when she was 24 years old (that explains the 'Jones' bit) and had four children. Tragically her entire family died of yellow fever. She moved to the city of Chicago and set up as a dressmaker. Then, in the huge Chicago fire of 1871, her business, along with thousands of others, was burned to the ground. Because it was ordinary working men and women who rebuilt Chicago, Mary felt they were owed a debt by the rich families who owned the city. She joined a trade union, which fought for fair wages for workers.

Now, when Mary Harris decided to fight, she fought like a demon. She began to travel across America helping out with strikes (where employees stopped working until

their pay and conditions were improved) and generally 'raising hell' (her own words) on behalf of workers.

In 1903 she tried to protect children from being exploited when she organised a protest against the horrible practice of using child labour in mills and mines. She brought hundreds of children on a march to the summer home of the US president, Theodore Roosevelt, in Oyster Bay in upstate New York. They carried banners reading 'We want to go to school not the mines'.

Mary refused to slow down as she got on in years and thus in old age became the white-haired 'Mother Jones'. She was the very best kind of agitator (political troublemaker): she only made trouble for the good of others and against employers who treated their workers very badly and paid them next to nothing for dangerous, back-breaking work. Once, when an American politician described her as 'the grandmother of all agitators', she replied, 'Yes, and I hope to live long enough to become the great-grandmother of all agitators!' That she most certainly did. She lived to the age of 93 and was still involved in trade union organisation in her 80s. As she neared the end of her life she advised her followers, 'Pray for the dead, and fight like hell for the living.'

Mary 'Mother Jones' Harris was a constant thorn in the side of some of the richest and most ruthless employers in America. She may have looked like your sweet old granny but, remember, looks can be deceptive.

PHOTO

NAME MARY JONES (NÉE HARRIS) AKA 'MOTHER JONES' (1837-1930)

OCCUPATION TRADE UNION ORGANISER

LIKELY TO SAY:	'Workers of the world unite.'
UNLIKELY TO SAY:	'Whatever you say, boss.'
LIKES:	Workers
DISLIKES:	Employers
CLAIM TO FAME:	Worked tirelessly on behalf of American workingmen and women

SHEILA McGUIGAN

After a hesitant start she finally got the hang of the bushranging lark.

DO YOU KNOW what a 'bushranger' is? No? Well, it's Australian English for an outlaw, or what used to be called a highwayman – someone who stopped you on the road at gunpoint and stole all your valuables.

By far the most famous Australian bushranger was Ned Kelly, who would often take on the police while wearing a suit of armour and a sort of bucket over his head so that they couldn't shoot him dead. Despite his name, he wasn't born in Ireland, but his father was.

Ned Kelly's female equivalent, however, was 100 per cent Irish. Her name, *as Gaeilge*, was Síle Ní Guig (Sheila McGuigan in English) and she was Australia's most famous female outlaw ... sorry, bushranger. She was driven to

thievery by poverty and by the need to feed her family. The McGuigans emigrated from a Gaeltacht (Irish-speaking) region in County Donegal to Australia in the 1860s. The family members spoke only Irish among themselves. That, however, posed a bit of a problem when Sheila began her career in crime. She would surprise her victims, confront them, hold them at gunpoint and holler, *'D'airgead nó do bheatha!'* ('Your money or your life!') When the first few bushranged clients stared back at her in bewilderment, she realised that, in order to avoid any misunderstandings about her intentions, she was going to have to learn some English. After she perfected her second language, her career as a bushranger really took off, until she was caught and jailed in 1875.

Sheila made good use of her time in prison,

however. While she was a convict, she studied law. When Sheila was released, she abandoned crime altogether and began to practise as a barrister. She was so successful that she made a very good living defending criminals, some of whom she had previously worked with. Partly because she was doing such a good job defending her clients (many of whom were as guilty as hell), the authorities appointed her as a judge in the Australian state of Victoria (Melbourne is the capital). She took to the bench (that's where judges sit) as readily as she had to bushranging and defending criminals. So much so that she became a justice of the Victorian Supreme Court, the highest court in the state, a decade before her death in 1916. Not bad for an Irish-speaking bushranger from rural Donegal.

Ever hear of the expression 'poacher turned gamekeeper'? It's meant to suggest someone who reforms and becomes an upstanding member of society. It might have been invented for Sheila McGuigan.

PHOTO

NAME SÍLE NÍ GUIG / SHEILA MCGUIGAN (1845-1916)

OCCUPATION(S) THIEF, BARRISTER, JUDGE

LIKELY TO SAY:	'Order in the court.'
LIKES:	The Irish language
DISLIKES:	Cheeky lawyers
CLAIM TO FAME:	Made the unique journey from criminal to Supreme Court justice

VIOLET GIBSON

Had she killed her intended victim, European history would have been different.

WHETHER SHE DID what she did because she hated dictators, or because she was mentally ill, or a bit of both, Violet Gibson almost did the world a huge favour on 7 April 1926 when she tried to shoot Benito Mussolini in Rome. Mussolini, known in Italy as 'Il Duce' (The Leader), was the head of the Italian Fascist movement, the evil and thuggish Blackshirts, and became Italian prime minister in 1922. He went on to become the main European ally of Hitler's Nazis during the Second World War. Had Violet's aim been just a little more accurate, Hitler and Germany might have had to take on the rest of Europe on their own.

Violet Gibson, born in Dublin, came from a well-off family. Her father was a wealthy barrister who was an Irish attorney general (that's the country's leading lawyer) under British rule and became Lord Ashbourne in 1885. Young Violet's mental health was never very strong, and in 1922 she experienced a period of emotional distress and was sent away to recover in a psychiatric hospital.

By 1926 she had apparently improved, was out of the hospital and was living in Italy. By then the country was ruled by the Blackshirt/Fascist party led by Mussolini. The Fascist leader was not very fond of the Italian system of democracy (in which the people were able to change their political leaders every four or five years). He was looking for an excuse to make sure that there would be no more elections and he could rule as a dictator. On 7 April 1926, Mussolini was walking, with his bodyguards,

around a *piazza* (a square) in Rome when Violet stepped in front of him and shot at him from an unreliable 30-year-old revolver. Just as she fired, Mussolini moved his head and the bullet merely grazed his nose. Undaunted, Violet tried again, but this time the vintage gun jammed.

As Mussolini was in the middle of an adoring crowd of supporters, Violet was lucky that she was not lynched (hanged) or beaten to death by an angry mob. The Italian police saved her from a horrible end. It quickly became clear to the Italian authorities that Violet had a mental health condition at the time of the attack. What might have tipped them off was her claim that an angel had kept her firing arm steady. If that was actually the case, she would hardly have missed!

Mussolini ordered that Violet be released into the care of the British government. This gesture made him look very good, and the attempt on his life aroused much sympathy in Italy, enabling him to make the changes he wanted in order to stay in power without the need for elections. Instead of ending his rule, Violet had played a part in helping Mussolini become the dictator he had always wanted to be.

Violet Gibson, 50 years old when she was deported to Britain, spent the last 30 years of her life in another psychiatric hospital. Despite almost killing one of the most evil men in European history, she was never released.

PHOTO

NAME VIOLET GIBSON
      (1876-1956)

OCCUPATION WOULD-BE ASSASSIN

UNLIKELY TO SAY:	'Viva Il Duce!'
LIKES:	Italy
DISLIKES:	Italian dictators
CLAIM TO FAME:	Attempted to assassinate Benito Mussolini in 1926

BARBARA RETZ

A Mormon, an Irish republican
and a German anti-Nazi – all in
the same person.

TECHNICALLY BARBARA BÖGER (her name before marriage) was not Irish, but she spent long enough living in Dublin to take an active part in the 1916 Rising and play an important role in the later War of Independence/Anglo-Irish War. She was doubly unusual in that she was also one of the few Irish members of the Church of Jesus Christ of the Latter-day Saints (more often known as the Mormons) in the early 20th century.

Babette (that's how she was generally known) was born in Stuttgart in Germany and arrived in Dublin as a teenager. The family had changed their name to Baker to allow the children to fit in a little better in Ireland. But Barbara fell in love with, and married, a butcher named George Retz. She ended up

with a German surname anyway. So, Barbara was both a butcher and a Baker. There is, however, no reason to believe that she was also a candlestick maker.

George owned two butcher's shops in Dublin. At the start of the First World War, feelings ran so high against Germany that one of the Retz shops was attacked by an angry mob. Because he was still a German citizen, George was taken away in 1914 by the British government and imprisoned on the Isle of Man along with dozens of other Germans living in Ireland. Barbara was left to run the family business on her own.

By 1916, the British authorities were probably wishing that they had sent Barbara to the prison camp on the Isle of Man along with George.

We don't know exactly what she got up to during the Rising of 1916 (apparently she was a friend of Patrick Pearse and that is why she was involved), but whatever it was, it was more than enough to get her arrested and thrown into Mountjoy jail with all the other women prisoners of Easter week.

That was not the end of her activities on behalf of the Irish independence, however. During the Anglo-Irish War (from 1919–21) a lot of young members of the IRA were 'on the run': they were being sought by the police and the British Army and had to hide out in a series of 'safe houses' run by their supporters all over the country. Barbara ran a Dublin safe house, at great risk to herself, and also supplied injured fighters with medicine. She must have been the most active German-born Irish republican in history.

Barbara didn't stop there. She was horrified by the rise of Adolf Hitler and the Nazis in her native Germany in the 1930s. In 1938, just before the start of the Second World War, she returned to Germany and courageously took part in demonstrations against the Nazis. Germans were executed or sent to concentration camps for far less. She was arrested and spent two weeks in jail. The British government managed to negotiate her release before anything really bad happened to her, so they must have got over their annoyance at the part she played in the 1916 Rising.

Jailed in Dublin after Easter week 1916, and then by Hitler's government, she must have been doing something right.

PHOTO

NAME BARBARA RETZ (NÉE BÖGER),
AKA BABETTE BAKER (1885-1948)

OCCUPATION(S) BUTCHER,
POLITICAL ACTIVIST

LIKELY TO SAY:	'Don't worry, it's safe as houses here.'
LIKES:	Meat, protecting people
DISLIKES:	Black and Tans, Nazis
CLAIM TO FAME:	Arrested by the British in 1916, and then by the Nazis in 1938

GEORGINA FROST

She took on the British state.
Result: Georgina 1, Britain 0.

NOWADAYS WE DON'T really have any jobs that can only be done by men. Anything a man can do, a woman can do – and should be paid the same for doing it. This, however, was not always the case. A century ago, there were very few occupations or professions that were open to women. They could be domestic servants, they could do factory work, at a pinch they could be teachers. This was especially the case in Ireland, where women were expected to be seen and not heard. Not Georgina Frost, however. Although she was a shy, retiring type, when it came to the world of work she was determined to be seen and heard. And what she achieved changed the world of work for women.

Georgina, known to all and sundry as 'Georgie', was a woman from Clare whose father worked as a legal clerk, running courtrooms in the towns of Sixmilebridge and Newmarket-on-Fergus. In carrying on his work he got a lot of help from his very efficient and capable daughter. In 1915, he decided that he wanted to retire. The local judges, known as magistrates, thought it made perfect sense for 'Georgie' to take over from her dad, but when the government discovered that 'Georgie' was a Georgina and not a George, they had a series of jumping-up-and-down fits. They insisted that such a delicate flower could not possibly fill such an arduous position. The Clare magistrates, who knew that Georgina had already been doing the job perfectly well for years, cried, 'Rubbish,' but they were overruled by important men in Dublin and London with big beards and bushy moustaches. (Facial hair was very popular at the time, though that might not be strictly relevant to the story.)

So, in order to keep her job, the 'delicate' Georgina took the British authorities in Dublin to court. She lost her case. The judge agreed with the 'moustaches' that she was far too frail and female for such challenging work (work that came pretty easily to Georgina). Unhappy with the first judgment, she appealed that verdict in a higher court. She lost that case too. Finally, she only had two options left: to give up, or to take her case all the way to the highest court in the United Kingdom (of which County Clare was a very reluctant part at the time). That was the House of Lords in London, where the beards and moustaches were absolutely splendid. Would she give up? Not likely. Not our Georgie.

When they realised that Georgina meant business and was planning to plead her case before the Lords, the British government caved in and changed the law. From then on, no woman could be prevented from taking up a government job because of her sex. Modest, frail, 'delicate' Georgina had toughed it out, taken on all that facial hair, won the day and changed the world for herself and thousands of other women.

Unfortunately, she didn't get to enjoy her triumph for long. Shortly after her victory, Ireland became independent and completely changed its court system. Georgina, once again, lost the job that she had fought so hard to keep. She got a pension from her former British employers and retired, but not before she had struck a huge blow for Irish (and British) women.

PHOTO

NAME GEORGINA FROST (1879–1939)

OCCUPATION CLERK OF COURT

UNLIKELY TO SAY:	'OK, I know when I'm beaten.'
LIKES:	Taking on the government
DISLIKES:	Being told she couldn't do her job because she was female
CLAIM TO FAME:	Won new rights from the British establishment for herself and future generations of women

TED AND MAUREEN SWEENEY

The two Mayopersons who aided the Allied
invasion of Europe in 1944.

WHEN THERE IS a storm brewing in the Atlantic, and the islands of Ireland and Britain are about to be pummelled by wind and rain (a very unusual occurrence I'm sure you'll agree!), the first place to know all about it is the west coast of Ireland. Someone who gets a bird's eye view of every single drop of Atlantic rain is the keeper of the Blacksod Bay lighthouse in Erris in the north of County Mayo. Blacksod Bay is bounded on its western side by the Mullet peninsula, famous for its weird haircuts. (Actually, that's completely untrue. It's really famous for its rugged beauty, something that cannot be said of the unrelated haircuts of the same name.)

In 1944 that (very windy) job was held by a man named Ted Sweeney. His wife, Maureen, ran the local post office and helped Ted out with weather readings. Both of them played an unexpected role in a key event of the Second World War.

During the Second World War, Ireland did not take sides in the conflict. However, the Irish government kept supplying Britain with weather reports. It was one of the Sweeney weather reports that caused the American supreme commander of the US and British forces, General Dwight Eisenhower, to abandon the landings planned for Normandy in France on 5 June 1944.

This was to be the first phase of the operation to take back France, Belgium and the Netherlands from Nazi Germany. But at 2 a.m. on 3 June, the Blacksod lighthouse reported an Atlantic storm over Mayo that would eventually reach the English Channel. If the Allies had stuck to their original plans, the storm would have caused havoc among the hundreds of boats carrying troops to the landing beaches.

Would it be safe to have a go on 6 June? Only if the invasion force got the all-clear. That's where Maureen came in. The only telephone in Blacksod Bay was at the post office. On 4 June, Maureen got a phone call from a woman in England who asked to speak to Ted. Ted was fetched and, in response to her question, he told the woman that, after days of continuous storms, there was finally going to be a brief break in the weather. When she rang back shortly afterwards to ask if he was *absolutely certain*, Ted and Maureen must have had some inkling that their weather report was very important indeed.

And they would have been right. After getting the all-clear from the Sweeneys, a relieved and grateful Eisenhower gave the order for the operation to begin. On 6 June, the invasion of France went ahead, marking the beginning of the end of the reign of terror of Nazi Germany in Europe.

And they couldn't have done it without Ted and Maureen Sweeney.

PHOTO

NAME TED AND MAUREEN SWEENEY

OCCUPATION(S) LIGHTHOUSE KEEPER (HIM),
                POSTMISTRESS (HER)

UNLIKELY TO SAY:	'Hello? Speaking! Yes, it's a soft day in Mayo.'
LIKES:	Meteorological equipment (him), friendly customers (her)
DISLIKES:	Being asked to double check barometer readings (him), awkward customers (her)
CLAIM TO FAME:	Helped avoid disaster during the Allied invasion of Europe

PART 3

UNACCLAIMED CREATIVES

If there is one thing we don't lack in Ireland it is famous 'creatives': writers, actors, musicians and painters who have become loved and celebrated all over the world. They've won Oscars, Emmys, Grammys, Nobel Prizes, the lot.

U2, Oscar Wilde, Eoin Colfer, Sinead O'Connor, James Joyce, Dustin the Turkey (OK, maybe not him).

Brendan Gleeson, Sally Rooney, Paul Mescal, W.B. Yeats (stop me whenever you want. I can go on to the bottom of the page and fill a few more after that).

Liam Neeson, Jessie Buckley, Kerry Condon, Niall Horan … Right, you probably get the point by now. We are famous for being good at 'the arts'.

Here are a few creatives who rarely get a mention. And, because we have so many thoroughly excellent performers and writers, I thought it might be a good idea to throw in a few who are well-liked despite not being all that good!

RACHAEL BAPTISTE CROW

The Irish mystery woman
who charmed musical audiences
as 'The Black Siren'.

SHE APPEARED OUT of nowhere in 1750. By 1773 she had disappeared again. No one knows exactly where she came from, or much about her, except that she was Irish. No one knows what happened to her when her musical career came to an end. Rachael Baptiste (sometimes written as Baptist) was a bit of a mystery woman who enthralled audiences at musical events and endured much prejudice as a Black woman. In 18th-century Ireland and Britain, being Black was associated with slavery. Many wealthy British and Irish families owned slaves who worked on plantations in the West Indies. Rachael persevered and overcame prejudice and bigotry with the beauty of her singing voice. She became famous and was known in Dublin as 'The Black Siren'.

She had been discovered by an Italian singing teacher, Bernardo Palma, who had moved to Dublin in the 1730s. In February 1750, at a Dublin concert organised to raise money for Palma, Rachael made her debut in front of Irish music lovers, being introduced to that audience as a 'native of this country'. For the next few years, she earned a living in Dublin performing in 'pleasure gardens' (places of entertainment where rich people would go for the evening to eat, drink and listen to music). Then, after six years of success, as suddenly as she had appeared, she disappeared!

What actually happened was that Rachael had decided to try her luck in England. She worked in London and in the famous summer resort of Bath, where Londoners would go to take advantage of the water (which had medicinal qualities that helped clear up some of their ailments – often caused by eating and drinking too much!). Rachael spent ten years touring around England, and at some point during that decade she was married to a music teacher by the name of Crow. He taught violin and guitar but also had a talent for restoring old paintings that had been damaged.

When she returned to Ireland she did so as Rachael Crow. Starting in Kilkenny in 1767, she and her husband spent a few months in a large Irish town every year. Rachael would perform while Mr Crow (we don't know what his first name was – sometimes even historians fail in their detective work) would teach. The couple spent the next six years in Ireland, finishing up with a winter in Belfast.

And then Rachael Baptiste Crow, the celebrated singer, was no more. Did she retire from the concert stage? Did she and her husband part company? Did she die a tragic death? Or did Mr and Mrs Crow simply up sticks and return to England? Good luck trying to find out. No one who has studied her life has ever been able to discover the truth.

But she was a truly remarkable figure in 18th-century Ireland and Britain. She succeeded in establishing a successful music career in a time of overwhelming racial prejudice.

PHOTO

NAME RACHAEL CROW (NÉE BAPTISTE) (MID- TO LATE-18TH CENTURY)

OCCUPATION CONCERT SINGER

LIKELY TO SING:	Anything from Irish airs to Handel
LIKES:	Who knows? She was a woman of mystery.
DISLIKES:	See above
CLAIM TO FAME:	Overcame prejudice to conquer the concert stage in Ireland and Britain

JAMES HOBAN

The Irishman who designed the White House, twice.

APART FROM HOUSING a lot of politicians, what does Leinster House in Dublin, the seat of our government, have in common with the White House in Washington DC, home of the president of the United States of America? Kilkenny man James Hoban, that's what. He emigrated to the USA at the age of 30 and became a successful architect. While he didn't design Leinster House, home of the Duke of Leinster, he stole some of the ideas that went into the creation of that building for his drawings of the White House.

James was from Callan, County Kilkenny and worked as a wheelwright (he made wheels for carriages) and a carpenter until he was in his twenties. However, he also showed a talent for drawing and was given a scholarship to a school in Dublin where he learned the basics of draughtsmanship (the making of technical drawings or designs). In 1785 he left for the USA, where they have 'draftsmanship' (Americans tend to spell things differently). He quickly established himself as an architect in the state of South Carolina. That was when he had a stroke of luck. He designed the main courthouse in the city of Charleston, South Carolina and the building was much admired by the first president of the USA, George Washington. When the decision was made to build a permanent home for the US president, Washington remembered James and encouraged him to enter the competition from which the final design would be chosen. James's drawings beat out eight other entries. His competitors included one of the country's 'Founding Fathers' (the men who drafted the US constitution),

Thomas Jefferson, who would go on to become president himself in 1801. So the Kilkenny man did well to beat off that sort of competition. He was selected as the White House architect and was invited to supervise the building of the president's new residence. This was done, mostly, with slave labour, as Washington DC was in the American south, where slavery continued until the end of the American Civil War in 1865. Some of the slaves belonged to James himself.

The finishing touch to the building came when the sandstone walls were whitewashed, otherwise it would have become known as the Grey House (actually, the *Gray* House, since that's how they spell the colour – sorry, the *color* – in the USA). The grey sandstone was from a quarry in nearby Virginia.

Once it was built, James must have thought he was finished with the White House. But he was wrong. In 1812, the USA went to war with Britain and in 1814 British troops set fire to the White House. James was brought back to start almost from scratch as only the shell of the building remained.

So not only did an Irishman design the White House, he did it twice.

PHOTO

NAME JAMES HOBAN
      (1755-1831)

OCCUPATION(S) ARCHITECT,
               WHEELWRIGHT,
               CARPENTER

LIKELY TO SAY:	'You want HOW MANY windows?'
LIKES:	Sandstone and whitewash
DISLIKES:	Fire-starting British soldiers
CLAIM TO FAME:	Designed the White House in Washington, DC

CATHERINE HAYES

She was known as
'The Swan of Erin' and
performed before royalty.

CATHERINE HAYES FROM Limerick was the most celebrated Irish soprano of her generation (as well as the generations before and after) yet she was as tough as they came. Once, on a concert tour of the American west, she took time off to head into the hills and pan for gold in the freezing rivers of the north California mountains! Yes, she was also a '49er' (someone who took part in the great California Gold Rush of 1849).

Catherine was an unbelievably popular singer, the Taylor Swift of her day. The difference being that, unlike Taylor, she didn't have to write her own songs. There were plenty of (mostly Italian) composers who were very happy to do that for her.

Her talent was recognised at an early age, and she trained with the best: a teacher named Manuel García in Paris. He had just tutored the most famous soprano (a singer whose voice can reach really high notes) of the 19th century, Jenny Lind, known as the 'Swedish Nightingale'. In order to raise enough money to pay for Catherine's travel and tuition, a concert was organised on her behalf in Limerick, and the proceeds were lodged into a bank account so that she could access the money when she needed it. Instead, Catherine withdrew the lot, stitched the cash into her underwear and headed for Paris with her mother!

Catherine was perfect for the operatic stage. She had an amazing vocal range and could cover two octaves and reach high D

(play it on the school piano then just try hitting that note yourself!). She could also act. When it comes to the acting part of opera, a lot of singers are about as good as the wooden boards they tread onstage. Catherine managed to make an opera's bad dialogue (which is almost always sung) sound believable.

Her reputation grew, and in 1849 she was invited to perform in Buckingham Palace before Queen Victoria. This was during the Great Famine in Ireland, where Britain was doing very little to help the starving Irish. Catherine sang a number of Italian operatic pieces for the English monarch and her 500 guests. The queen asked for an encore when the recital ended. With a knowing grin, Catherine abandoned Italian opera and sang one of the great 'Irish' ballads of the 19th century, 'Kathleen Mavourneen' (it's not actually an Irish song, but that's another story) just to remind her upper-class English audience of who she was, where she came from and what was happening in Ireland.

Catherine had a short but successful career (she died at the early age of 42) but she travelled the world in that time, singing in the USA, South America, Australia and India. She sang to royalty and to humble miners (when she wasn't panning for gold herself). She was also the first Irish performer to sing at the world-famous La Scala opera house in Milan and at the Royal Opera House in London.

Taylor Swift, eat your heart out!

PHOTO

NAME CATHERINE HAYES, AKA CATERINA HAYEZ (1818–1861)

OCCUPATION OPERA SINGER

UNLIKELY TO SAY:	'I should have stuck to prospecting.'
LIKES:	Italian composers
DISLIKES:	Lousy tenors who couldn't act
CLAIM TO FAME:	The most famous Irish soprano of the 19th century

LOLA MONTEZ

A dancer who was famous
for being famous.

THE FIRST THING you should know about Lola Montez is that you shouldn't accept anything you read about her at face value. You simply cannot trust anything she ever said about herself. She probably lied about her age, her place of birth and even her name. And that was just the easy stuff! When she started telling stories about her wild and exciting life, chances were that some of them were just that, stories. Porky-pies. Fascinating, but total fantasy. Having said that, the stuff that was definitely not made up was still pretty amazing.

Lola Montez was the stage name of (probably) Sligo-born Eliza Rosanna Gilbert. Though she might have been born in Limerick, as that's what she told people. Oddly, she claimed to be older than she was, or perhaps she wasn't sure herself. Her gravestone (in New York) claims that she was born in 1818. But her baptismal certificate shows that she was actually born three years later, in 1821. When most people lie about their age it's to make themselves appear to be younger. Not our Lola.

She dreamed up the stage name 'Lola Montez', probably because it sounded a bit more interesting than 'Eliza Gilbert'. That was the name she then used throughout her dancing career.

Lola's fame as a performer, and her natural beauty, brought her to the attention of many powerful men all across Europe. One was the French author Alexandre Dumas, writer of the adventure novel *The Three Musketeers*. Another was Tsar Nicholas I of Russia.

Then there was King Ludwig I of Bavaria. He fell head over heels in love with Lola and she lived with him until the people of Bavaria got tired of her antics (they said she had too much power and influence over their king) and kicked her out.

When things got too hot for Lola in Europe, she did what a lot of Irish people tended to do and headed for the USA. There she restarted her career as a dancer and was very much in demand in music halls all across the country. This was because of her 'Tarantula Dance', which involved pretending that a spider had got loose in her clothing. Frankly, Lola was no great shakes as a dancer, but her audiences didn't seem to mind one bit. Theatre critics ran scared of giving her performances a bad review. That's because she beat one of them with a horsewhip and challenged another to a duel for writing mean things about her!

You did not mess with Lola Montez.

PHOTO

NAME ELIZA ROSANNA GILBERT, AKA LOLA MONTEZ (1821–1861)

OCCUPATION DANCER

LIKELY TO SAY:	'Don't you know who I am?'
LIKES:	Men with titles (king, tsar and suchlike)
DISLIKES:	Anyone who got in her way
WEAPON OF CHOICE:	The horsewhip
CLAIM TO FAME:	She was (briefly) one of the most famous women in the world.

JOHN WALLACE CRAWFORD

Was 'Captain Jack' Crawford the worst poet in the world?

THE COUNTY OF **Donegal has produced more than its share of great Irish writers. Probably the best known is Brian Friel, who wrote a number of plays that were works of pure genius, like *Dancing at Lughnasa*, or *Philadelphia, Here I Come*, and who lived in Donegal for much of his life.**

But the county also has to accept responsibility for John Wallace 'Jack' Crawford (although his parents were Scottish, so the Scots can take some of the blame). He emigrated from Carndonagh in County Donegal at the age of 14 and his work was as far from being 'pure genius' as the Inishowen Peninsula is from his stomping

ground in the American west. That was where he earned a reputation as an army scout and a journalist (at the same time!) during the so-called 'Indian Wars' of the 1870s. Among the men he befriended was William 'Buffalo Bill' Cody, a legend of the 'Wild West' who earned his nickname by killing hundreds of buffalo (bison), an animal vital to the survival of the Native American nations of the American west. So devoted was Jack to Buffalo Bill that he once brought him a bottle of whiskey that he'd carried for 300 miles without drinking a single drop. But then, Jack was unusual among journalists and soldiers: he was a teetotaller (someone who does not drink alcohol), and he never touched a drop of the stuff in his life.

In the 1890s, Jack put his experiences in the Indian Wars to good use when he became an entertainer, dazzling audiences with:

Tales of bravery and derring-do,
Some of which might even have been true.

See what I did there? I wrote a Captain Jack poem! That's the name he went by as he performed for audiences across the USA. They would often turn out in their thousands to hear his tall tales. Because, whatever about his abilities as a writer, Crawford was certainly a popular performer and a terrific storyteller.

He wrote seven books of verse, most of which was just as bad as my feeble effort above. He also wrote more than a hundred short stories and four plays, all about his experiences as an army scout in the American Wild West, working as a sort of navigator for regiments of US cavalry (soldiers mounted on horseback).

You want some proof of just how bad his poetry was? This is a verse of a poem written about the death of a miner in a camp somewhere in the Black Hills of Dakota:

Only a miner killed!
Bury him quick.
Just write his name
On a piece of stick.

Now do you believe me? It's not exactly Shakespeare. But his prose is a lot better, otherwise he would never have made a living as a journalist.

NAME JOHN WALLACE CRAWFORD, AKA 'CAPTAIN JACK' (1847-1917)

OCCUPATION COWBOY POET

UNLIKELY TO SAY:	'Shorry, Bill. I dhrank all the fwiskey.'
LIKES:	Finding words to rhyme with 'buffalo'
DISLIKES:	Blank verse (poems that don't rhyme)
CLAIM TO FAME:	Possibly the worst poet in the world. Ever!

AMANDA McKITTRICK ROS

Does she deserve the title of 'Worst Novelist Ever'?

THE WRITER KNOWN as Amanda McKittrick Ros, from County Down, once said that she would 'be talked about at the end of a thousand years'. As it happens this was one of her few readable and sensible sentences. However, given that she died in 1939, and I am writing about her almost a century later, she might not have been completely wrong. But if people are still discussing her work 900 years from now it won't be because of how good it was: it will be on account of its hideous awfulness. Because Amanda McKittrick Ros (she basically just dropped an 's' from her real surname to come up with her pen name – not very imaginative) was the queen of something called 'purple prose'. This is a style of writing that starts by being completely over the top and then goes from there to heights of unimaginable purplitude (that's not actually a word, but when writing about Amanda, I figure I can get away with it).

So, I hear you asking, if she was that bad, how come someone was prepared to pay good money to publish her work? The simple answer is that she had a doting husband, Andrew Ross, who was the stationmaster of Larne railway station. On their tenth wedding anniversary, in 1897, he wanted to give her a very special present, so he paid to have her first novel published. It was a romantic work entitled *Irene Iddesleigh* and it was a laugh a page.

The problem was that *Irene Iddesleigh* was not supposed to be funny. It was described by the great American writer Mark Twain as 'one of the greatest unintentionally humorous novels of all time'. One critic said that on reading the book he 'shrank before it in tears and terror'. The bould Amanda responded by claiming that the critic was secretly in love with her. Don't you just envy someone with that amount of self-confidence? She always believed that the people who reviewed her book were not smart enough to see her great talent.

Your next question will probably be 'Right, so that was it then – surely she only got to publish one lousy novel?' Well ... not exactly. You see, *Irene Iddesleigh* was one of those rarities: it was so bad that it was good. People wanted to see if she could outdo herself the second time around with something that was even worse. She duly obliged with *Delina Delaney*. She claimed it sold so many copies that she was able to build a house with the proceeds. Maybe it was a doll's house?

One of her works that was (thankfully) never published was called *Six Months in Hell*, probably so-called because that's what it felt like to read it.

SUSAN AND ELIZABETH YEATS

They had to step out from the shadows of two famous brothers.

THERE ARE TWO exceptionally famous members of the Yeats family of Sandymount in Dublin. William Butler Yeats was Ireland's most famous poet (until Seamus Heaney). He founded the Abbey Theatre in the 1890s and won the Nobel Prize for Literature in 1923. His brother was Jack Butler Yeats, a famous artist who, in 1924, won an Olympic silver medal for painting (I kid you not) and became the first Olympic medallist of the new Irish Free State.

None of which left much room for their sisters, Susan and Elizabeth. In fact, one famous reference to them was very uncomplimentary indeed. In the great Irish novel *Ulysses*, the author, James Joyce, refers to Susan and Elizabeth (without naming them) as 'the weird sisters'. If you know anything about James Joyce (he was quite odd) you might be tempted to say, 'That's good, coming from him!' Joyce was probably influenced by the very male feeling in the early 20th century against women who did not marry or have children, but who chose to have careers instead. That was enough to make them 'weird'. In the 16th century, they probably would have been accused of witchcraft and burned at the stake.

Known as 'Lily' (Susan) and 'Lolly' (Elizabeth), the Yeats sisters were far from weird. Life was not easy for them as children.

Their father, John Butler Yeats, fancied himself as an artist but lacked the skill to make a decent living. Forced to fend for themselves, Lily became an embroiderer and Lolly trained as a teacher. From the early 1900s they both lived together in a house in Churchtown in suburban Dublin, but never got on all that well with one another. Lolly went into printing and worked on some of brother Willy's poetry books, constantly giving out to him about his sloppy handwriting, spelling and punctuation. Then, in 1907, she and Lily set up their own company, Cuala Press, the only Irish publishing firm run by women, which also employed only women. For years they produced volumes of poetry and stories, often with absolutely stunning illustrations, while they fought with each other and with their more famous brothers (who, in fairness, put a lot of their own work, and money, into Cuala Press).

Lolly died first, leaving Lily to run the show as she saw fit. However, Lolly had the last word at her sister's funeral in Churchtown in 1949. As the funeral got underway, Lily's coffin fell over. Her relatives believed that this was a sign from Lolly – even in death, she was still the boss.

PHOTO

NAME SUSAN 'LILY' YEATS (1866-1949), ELIZABETH 'LOLLY' YEATS (1868-1940)

OCCUPATION(S) PRINTERS AND PUBLISHERS

LEAST FAVOURITE SONG:	'We are family' ('I got all my sisters with me')
LIKES:	Arts and crafts
DISLIKES:	Each other
CLAIM TO FAME:	Started the only Irish publishing company run entirely by women

ARTHUR SHIELDS

The show didn't go on,
because actor Arthur Shields
had a gun and a mission.

ARTHUR SHIELDS BELONGED to a family of working-class Protestants from Dublin. He left school at 14 and took up acting a few years later, eventually joining the famous Abbey Theatre group (based in Abbey Street in Dublin). He also joined the Irish Volunteers, led by Patrick Pearse, and took part in the 1916 Rising. His absence from an Abbey Theatre play on Easter Monday 1916 was one of the problems that led to its cancellation ... although the fact that there was a rebellion going on a hundred metres away probably had something to do with it as well. After the Rising, Arthur was marched off with the other Volunteer prisoners to the famous Frongoch internment camp in north Wales, where he started ... go on, guess ... yes, a drama society.

He went back to the Abbey after his release, then in 1936 was invited over to Hollywood by the great film director John Ford. Ford was making a movie version of the play *The Plough and the Stars* (written by Seán O'Casey, another working-class Dublin Protestant) and wanted Arthur to play the part of Patrick Pearse. Arthur might only have been a foot soldier in the Rising itself, but in Hollywood he got to play the man who read the 1916 Proclamation and led the rebellion!

Over the course of a long career, Arthur, although he was not a Roman Catholic, played a lot of Catholic priests. This, as well as playing policemen, was a fate experienced by many Irish actors in the USA, including Arthur's older and much

J. FORD

more famous brother, William, who also lived and worked in America (under the stage name Barry Fitzgerald). William even won an Oscar for Best Supporting Actor in 1944 when he co-starred as a priest in a film called *Going My Way.*

Arthur had always meant to move back home, but due to a series of unfortunate accidents – breaking a leg in New York, then catching tuberculosis, which meant he had to live in a warmer climate – he never managed it. So he must have been pleased when John Ford cast him as a Church of Ireland rector and brought him back to Ireland for a bit in 1951 to make the film *The Quiet Man*, which went on to become one of the most famous (and beloved) films ever shot in Ireland.

In 1941, Ford cast Arthur in the film *How Green Was My Valley*, which led to an amazing coincidence: Ford had also cast English actor John Loder, whose real name was John Lowe and who, in 1916, had been a British Army lieutenant. John had served under his father, General William Lowe, commanding officer of the British Army in Dublin, and helped put down the Easter rebellion. When Patrick Pearse surrendered to General Lowe, John stood alongside his father and looked on. In 1916 they would happily have shot each other, but 25 years later, John sat alongside Arthur, one of Pearse's Volunteers, to read through a film script. And this time, Arthur had the much bigger role!

NINETTE DE VALOIS

The Wicklow-born ballerina who established the Royal Ballet in London.

WHEN YOU'RE TOLD that someone with a name like de Valois is Irish, your first reaction is probably not going to be 'Ah, yes, she must one of the Tubbercurry de Valoises!' And in fact, the real name of the great ballet dancer and producer Ninette de Valois was Edris Stannus (of the Blessington, County Wicklow, Stannuses. Come on, you must know them!). She adopted her more French-sounding stage name in 1913 when it was clear that she was destined to be a ballerina.

While she did not have a long career as a professional dancer (she had to give up in the early 1920s because of the after-effects of childhood polio), Ninette made a huge contribution to ballet in the 20th century. She became a choreographer (the person who dictates how the dancers move around the stage) and then founded her own ballet company in London, employing a number of dancers. She became what is known in the theatre world as an 'impresario' – someone who raises money to produce work on stage. In her case that was famous and much-loved ballet productions, especially Russian classics like Tchaikovsky's *Sleeping Beauty*, *Swan Lake* or *The Nutcracker*.

Ninette's family left Wicklow when she was seven years old but she returned to Ireland frequently in the 1920s and 1930s to work with the great Irish poet W.B. Yeats,

who ran the Abbey Theatre. They worked together on the dance moves for a number of his plays. She also set up a ballet school in the Abbey Theatre. After 1940, though, she must have had mixed feelings about ever coming back to Ireland again as much of the land around the house her family had owned in Blessington, known as Baltiboys, was submerged under millions of gallons of water to create the Poulaphouca Reservoir.

Most of Ninette's work was in London, where, from 1931, her ballet company was based in an old restored theatre called Sadler's Wells, located in the north of the city. She also took the Sadler's Wells Ballet company abroad, visiting the USA almost every year from 1949, and touring Europe as well. In 1940, de Valois and her dancers barely made it out of the Netherlands before the Germans took over the country at the beginning of the Second World War.

In 1956, the newly crowned Queen Elizabeth II, who had become English monarch three years before, issued what is known as a royal charter to the Sadler's Wells Ballet company, which then became the Royal Ballet. Seven years later Ninette formally 'retired' but no one really believed that she was finished with ballet. As she approached her 100th birthday in 1998 (you'll see from her dates that she lived in three different centuries) Ninette was still interested and involved in the running of the Royal Ballet and was still attending performances.

While Ireland is hardly Russia when it comes to the art of ballet (Russian dancers, composers and choreographers are world-famous) at least one Irish person, Ninette de Valois from Wicklow, had a huge impact on the world of ballet. Not many people know that. But now you do.

PHOTO

NAME EDRIS STANNUS,
AKA NINETTE DE VALOIS
(1898-2001)

OCCUPATION(S) DANCER,
CHOREOGRAPHER,
THEATRE IMPRESARIO

UNLIKELY TO SAY:	'I hate Swan Lake.'
LIKES:	W.B. Yeats
DISLIKES:	A sloppy jeté (that's an acrobatic ballet move)
CLAIM TO FAME:	The founder of what, in 1956, became the Royal Ballet

DELIA MURPHY

She was a famous singer,
but also a quiet saviour
of many lives.

TO MOST IRISH PEOPLE of a certain age, Delia Murphy was a famous Irish ballad singer from Mayo who had a number of big hits in the 1930s and 1940s ('The Blackbird' and 'The Spinning Wheel'). She had a very unusual voice, was very popular and recorded over 100 songs. In her youth, she befriended members of the Travelling community on her father's land. It was from them that she learned many of the ballads she made famous.

If that is all there was to Delia Murphy, however, she would probably not have been included in this book. But there was another mysterious 'cloak and dagger' side to her. She had a secret life in the 1940s that she could not talk about. She was a genuine hero who courageously put herself in huge danger to help hundreds of distressed people whose own lives were in peril.

Delia was able to do this because, at the age of 22, she married an Irish diplomat, Thomas Kiernan. His job was to represent Ireland abroad. In 1941, he became ambassador to the Vatican, a small independent state in the middle of Rome where the pope lives. Like Ireland, the Vatican remained neutral during the Second World War, while the Italian dictator Benito Mussolini (the one Violet Gibson tried to shoot) took the side of Nazi Germany. When Mussolini was deposed by his own people in 1943, the Germans took over Italy. Rome was now a very dangerous place for Jews, who were being sent in their thousands from all over Europe to Nazi concentration camps.

It was almost as dangerous for American and British soldiers who escaped from German prisoner-of-war camps.

Delia refused to stand by and see good and innocent people murdered by the cruel and evil Nazi regime. She found a useful ally in a daring Irish priest, Monsignor Hugh O'Flaherty. Between them, they managed to smuggle hundreds of endangered people into safe houses all over Rome and eventually get them to safety. Had either of them been caught, there is no telling what the Nazis would have done with them, even though Delia was married to an Irish ambassador. Rather than endanger her husband, she did not tell him of the work she and Hugh O'Flaherty were doing, although some of the escapees were smuggled to safety past Nazi checkpoints in the boot of Tom Kiernan's car!

Thankfully both Delia and Hugh O'Flaherty survived the war. She did not have to act out, at the hands of the Nazis at least, the title of one of her most popular songs, 'I'll Live 'til I Die'.

PHOTO

NAME DELIA MURPHY
(1902–1971)

OCCUPATION SINGER

LIKELY TO SAY:	'Don't worry, we'll get you out of here.'
LIKES:	People who needed her help
DISLIKES:	Nazis
CLAIM TO FAME:	Assisted hundreds of Jews and others in their escape from Italy in the Second World War

DICK FARRELLY

The solitary bus journey that
produced an Irish musical classic.

IT'S IRONIC THAT one of the greatest Irish songs about exile and emigration was written by a man with a steady job who never had to leave Ireland to make a living. Dick Farrelly, born in Kells, County Meath in 1916, spent most of his working life as a member of An Garda Síochána in a variety of Garda stations around Ireland. He was fortunate that he was able to remain in his native country at a time when many hundreds of thousands of Irish people were forced to leave to seek employment abroad.

Dick, a very quiet and gentle man, was doubly fortunate in that he also had an enormous talent for music, as both a performer and a songwriter. He wrote a number of hit songs in the 1950s and '60s but will always be remembered for one in particular, 'The Isle of Innisfree', a song about longing for homeland, which begins with the line, 'I've met some folks who say that I'm a dreamer ...'

One fateful evening in 1950, Dick was on the bus from his native Kells, returning to work in Dublin. As the bus travelled along the road to Navan a hauntingly beautiful melody popped into his head. Nowadays he would simply have risked some funny looks from his fellow passengers and hummed the notes into his phone. Back then he didn't even have a pen and paper to record the melody. All he could do to avoid losing the song was to hum it to himself over and over again as the bus, achingly slowly, approached Dublin. As he did so, a sense of dread rose within him. What if someone was to sit down beside him and start a conversation about the weather?

Fortunately, no one did and the song was not lost to a chatterbox. Two years later 'The Isle of Innisfree' became an international hit when it was recorded by the silken-voiced American crooner and film star Bing Crosby, who was always on the lookout for good material.

It got even better after that. The great Hollywood film director John Ford was planning to shoot a movie in Ireland that year called *The Quiet Man*, starring John Wayne and Maureen O'Hara (and Arthur Shields!). Ford heard the song, loved it and wanted it in his film. It was played over the opening credits and used in brief snatches almost a dozen times on the soundtrack, which was written by the award-winning film music composer Victor Young. Sadly, only Young ever got any credit for the music of *The Quiet Man* (including a Golden Globe award nomination).

Dick had the last laugh, however. When Steven Spielberg made his wonderful film *ET: The Extra-Terrestrial* in 1982, he used a 30-second clip from *The Quiet Man* in one of the scenes. Underneath the image of John Wayne kissing Maureen O'Hara, you could hear some of *The Quiet Man* theme music, but the melody was from 'The Isle of Innisfree', which meant that Dick was entitled to a hefty royalty payment.

Take that, Victor Young!

PHOTO

NAME RICHARD 'DICK' FARRELLY (1916-1990)

OCCUPATION(S) GARDA SÍOCHÁNA, COMPOSER

LIKELY TO SAY:	'I've met some folks who say that I'm a dreamer.'
LIKES:	Dreaming up words and music (but not while on patrol)
DISLIKES:	Victor Young
CLAIM TO FAME:	Writer of the classic Irish song 'The Isle of Innisfree'

PART 4

UNSUNG GENIUSES

You don't necessarily have to be a scientist to be an inventor. The great Italian Leonardo da Vinci was an artist, but he still managed to produce drawings and designs for all sorts of amazing contraptions. Sometimes, as in the case of Harry Ferguson from County Down – who built his own airplane and car before developing the tractor into something a farmer could use to plough a field – they were called 'mad mechanics'. That was because they would tinker with anything to make it work better; to get it to do something different; or just for the sake of it to see what would happen. Most of us, when we take things apart and put them back together again, manage to leave out a few bits and bobs and are left wondering what they are for. Are they really necessary? (Trust me, they are.) Will the hair dryer work without this cog? (It won't.)

Hats off to our nine unsung Irish geniuses. At least you'll be able to give them the credit they so richly deserve.

RICHARD POEKRICH

The inventor of the
musical instrument that was
'away with the angels'.

I N SPITE OF the unusual surname, Richard Poekrich (sometimes known as Puckeridge) actually came from County Monaghan. He took over the family estate in 1722 and lost most of his inheritance in a variety of hare-brained schemes. Even with some of the more sensible schemes (he owned a brewery), he was never quite able to turn them into a success. It's hard not to make a go of selling beer in Ireland, but Richard managed it. Let's face it, even if he'd started a beer business in Germany (they like their beer even more than we do) he still probably wouldn't have been able to make money.

He also had a lot of good ideas that he was not able to do much about because he was so far ahead of his time. These included the idea of giving people blood transfusions. However, he was a bit off the wall with this one. He saw transfusions as the key to a much longer life, rather than as a solution to severe blood loss. He didn't think, however, that people should be allowed to live forever. He believed that anyone making use of other people's blood to extend their own lives should not be allowed to continue beyond the age of 999! Good luck with that. Linking up the Liffey and the Shannon rivers with a series of canals was another one of his bright notions. He was also convinced that boats made of metal would be able to float (I wonder whatever came of that idea).

Not so smart was his prediction that, one day, human beings would sprout wings and be able to fly. He also put forward a proposal

to grow grapevines (for making wine) on Irish bogs. Maybe we missed a trick there. Perhaps Bórd na Móna could have been turning out bottles of Chateau Briquette rather than turf all these years.

Richard's lasting achievement was in developing something he called the 'angelic organ'. This was a line of glasses, each of which produced a different note when the player wet their finger and stroked the top of each in a circular motion (you can try this one at home, just put different amounts of water in each glass). His new instrument was a big hit with audiences in Ireland and England, and Richard could play most of the classical favourites of the day on it.

Sadly, Richard came to an unpleasant end. He died in a fire in a restaurant in London. But his invention lived after him and some composers even wrote pieces for his strange glassy instrument.

PHOTO

NAME RICHARD POEKRICH (OR PUCKERIDGE) (1697-1759)

OCCUPATION(S) MUSICIAN, INVENTOR, PRETTY ROTTEN POET (THOUGH NOT AS BAD AS CAPTAIN JACK)

LIKELY TO SAY:	'Whee, I can fl–'
LIKES:	Glasses (the kind you drink out of)
DISLIKES:	Being in debt
CLAIM TO FAME:	Inventor of a very strange musical instrument

WILLIAM PARSONS

He built 'Leviathan', once the biggest telescope in the world.

THERE AREN'T MANY Irish claims to world records that have stood for over 70 years. That distinction belongs to a wondrous creation, the 'Leviathan'. It was named after an enormous biblical sea serpent that enjoyed snacking on unwary sailors and supposedly had around half a dozen heads. The excess number of heads suggests that it was probably a myth: most creatures (including we humans) are perfectly happy with single-headedness.

The Irish Leviathan, however, was definitely not mythological. It was so named because of its vast size but it lived harmlessly in the grounds of Birr Castle in County Offaly, posing no threat to seafarers or landlubbers alike. Leviathan was (and still is) an enormous telescope designed and built in the 1840s by William Parsons, the 3rd Earl of Rosse, owner of Birr Castle. Back then, the town of Birr was called after his family: it was known as Parsonstown.

William was a mathematician and astronomer who liked to build his own telescopes. He tried to outdo himself each time by creating something bigger and better. For example, in the late 1830s he built a telescope that was 36 inches (90 cm) wide before scrapping that for Leviathan, which was twice as big at 72 inches (1.8 m) wide. It weighed 16 tons. Leviathan was so big that Rosse claimed a man wearing a top hat could walk through it. He later went on to prove this ... by having a man wearing a top hat walk through it!

Because telescope builders were notoriously tight when it came to information about their creations, William had to build Leviathan more or less from scratch, making it up as he went along.

Crab Nebula

Whirlpool Galaxy

When he finished the telescope in 1845, he trained his new toy on the stars to sketch distant spiral galaxies and to study nebulae (clouds of dust and gas in space). The galaxies looked like brightly lit waterspouts; in fact, one that he studied closely was later called the Whirlpool Galaxy. He also named the famous Crab Nebula because he thought it looked like a ... well, you probably don't need me to explain that one.

William's life was made all the more lively by his rivalry with an English scientist, John Herschel, with whom he had many debates and spats about astronomy. When it came to science, these two men didn't see eye to eye on an awful lot. But John Herschel never built a telescope that was the largest in the world for 72 years (in 1917 the Mount Wilson Observatory in California built the Hooker Telescope, which was 100 inches wide). So, 1–0 to William.

Any time you want to see Leviathan you can visit it in the beautiful grounds of Birr Castle. It's still an extraordinary piece of design and engineering. But you probably won't be allowed to walk through it wearing a top hat. Which is a shame really.

PHOTO

NAME WILLIAM PARSONS, 3RD EARL OF ROSSE (1800–1867)

OCCUPATION(S) LANDLORD, MEMBER OF PARLIAMENT, ASTRONOMER, HUMANITARIAN

UNLIKELY TO SAY:	'Ah, go on. Have a look for the Man in the Moon.'
LIKES:	Stargazing and telescopes
DISLIKES:	John Herschel
CLAIM TO FAME:	Designed and built the largest telescope in the world

JOHN TYNDALL

The man who explained why the sky is blue.

WHEN, IN 1859, Carlowman John Tyndall worked out the connection between the release of carbon dioxide (CO2) into the atmosphere and the warming of planet Earth, it wasn't such a big deal as it is now. Back then there weren't as many people around to burn coal or wood, and no one had started using oil in the ways it is used today. John might as well have discovered that he could juggle a couple of tennis balls (try it, it's not that hard). So, not that much notice was taken of his discovery and he became famous for something completely different.

John was one of those people who seemed to be good at just about everything (I know, I hate them too). In addition to making a number of scientific discoveries, he was also a famous mountaineer. From 1856 onwards he would visit the Alps every year, and in 1861 was a member of the team that was first to climb a 4,506-metre peak called the Weisshorn. Just in case any of his very serious scientific colleagues thought of this as trivial timewasting, while he was up there he did some amazing research, just for fun, on Alpine glaciers ... as you would! He has three glaciers and three mountains named after him in North America, South America and Australia. But even that is not what he's most famous for.

Had John been alive at the right time he could have won a Nobel Prize in Physics for a wide variety of work, or, at the very least, he could have become Carlowman of the Year. But neither honour existed during his lifetime. When he began his career as a scientist, he was best known for his work on heat.

In the 1860s, however, he began to do experiments with light. Using a simple glass tube with a white light at one end (acting as the sun), he filled the tube with smoke and noticed that, from the side, it looked blue. John was aware that white light was actually made up of a number of different colours. Ever seen a rainbow? That is actually white light split into its different colours by the sun shining through rainfall. John figured out from his observations that the colour of the sky is caused by the blue light from the sun scattering around particles in the Earth's upper atmosphere. The result became known as the Tyndall Effect. This is one experiment you can definitely try at home. Get a glass of water and a torch. Shine the torch through the water while stirring in a couple of drops of milk. What do you see?

The colour Tyndall Blue is also called after him, which is waaaay cooler than having mountains and glaciers bearing your name. They should really award him a posthumous (after death) Nobel Prize. Or Carlowman of the Year.

PHOTO

NAME   JOHN TYNDALL
       (1820-1893)

OCCUPATION   SCIENTIST

LIKELY TO SAY:	'Darn, grey skies again.'
LIKES:	The colour blue
DISLIKES:	Mountains he couldn't climb
CLAIM TO FAME:	Discovered why the sky is blue (when it's not covered over by clouds)

MARY WARD

This amazing scientist is, sadly, remembered for all the wrong reasons.

MARY WARD WAS cat-like in her curiosity. She loved to find out how things worked. Sadly it was this interest in nature, science and machines that led to her death at the very early age of 42. She grew up in Ferbane, County Offaly and was encouraged by her parents in her enthusiasm for collecting and drawing insects. She built up a huge collection of images of all sorts of creatures and catalogued them (listed their names) very diligently.

Probably her most impressive work was when she made a number of sketches of Leviathan, the giant telescope in Birr Castle, designed and built by her cousin William Parsons, 3rd Earl of Rosse – the one that you read about a few pages ago (unless you're skipping forward!). Mary, who was just as fascinated by astronomy as zoology, made a lot of use of her cousin's magnificent creation to look at the distant stars.

But it was with a much smaller lens, designed to examine objects only a few centimetres away, that she really made her reputation as a scientist. In her teens Mary was given her first microscope and never looked back ... but she did spend a lot of time looking through the lens at magnified images of flora and fauna. Even though she wasn't allowed to attend university (because she was female) that did not stop her writing a book in 1858 about her findings. It was called *Sketches with the Microscope*. The book was a runaway success and editions were still being published a decade after her death.

Had Mary been a little less curious she might have lived long enough to see her own girls

A WORLD of WONDERS REVEALED BY THE MICROSCOPE

THE TELESCOPE BY M WARD

(she had eight children) go to university when, towards the end of the 19th century, third-level colleges began to accept female students. Sadly it was not to be, and it was her inventor cousin, William Parsons, who played a major role in her death. Parsons had developed a steam-driven car, which was rather like a train engine that did not run on rails. When, shortly after their father's death, two of the Earl of Rosse's sons offered Mary a ride on his new contraption, she accepted immediately, eager to try out any new invention. However, when the car came to a sharp bend, Mary was thrown out of the vehicle. The wheels of the steam car then ran over her, killing her instantly.

Mary Ward, while she is remembered for her contribution to science in the 19th century, was also, sadly, believed to be the first victim of a road traffic accident in the world.

PHOTO

NAME MARY WARD
(1827–1869)

OCCUPATION(S) BOTANIST, ASTRONOMER

UNLIKELY TO SAY:	'Is that a Red admiral?'
LIKES:	Collecting insects
DISLIKES:	Universities that would not accept women students
CLAIM TO FAME:	An amazing scientist but is also remembered for her tragic death

JOHN PHILLIP HOLLAND

The original submarine was supposed to be used against English ships.

YOU MIGHT BE surprised to learn that the man who invented the submarine was brought up speaking only Irish. And that he was once a member of the Christian Brothers. He also survived the Great Famine of the 1840s in a part of the country, County Clare, that witnessed thousands of deaths.

John Phillip Holland left Ireland for the USA when he was in his early thirties. In his pocket was a rough plan for a boat that could operate under water. He got plenty of time to work on his new project as he slipped in an icy Boston street and broke his leg shortly after arriving in America. He was very excited about his new invention, but when he showed his design to the US Navy, they yawned and said 'Next'.

Although the US Navy was ridiculously short-sighted about John's idea, his brother Michael could see the potential. As it happened, Michael was a member of the Irish-American revolutionary organisation the Fenian Brotherhood, who were plotting to set up an Irish republic, independent of Britain. The potential for what, you might ask? Good question. The potential for blowing up British ships in a war to win Irish independence. That potential! British naval shipping would be at a bit of a disadvantage if their warships could be sunk by an enemy they couldn't even see.

For the next six years, John worked hard on his invention – he also came up with the name 'submarine' to describe it. He was funded by money that had originally been collected by the Fenians to buy dynamite to blow up targets in Britain. The Fenians reckoned that John's research was just as good an investment as explosives. John's submarine was capable of causing far more damage to Britain than a few sticks of dynamite, although they went ahead and bought those anyway, just in case. This was just as well, really, because even though John managed to develop a submarine – he called it *The Fenian Ram* – it didn't work too well. He eventually fell out with the Fenians, who proved to be just as short-sighted as the US Navy and decided to stick to dynamite. (No, not literally!)

Even without the dynamite money, John kept plugging away at his invention. It went from being 30 to 53 feet long, and in 1900, on his sixth attempt at building a submarine, he came up with a vessel that had a six-man crew, could remain underwater for two days and could fire torpedoes. Was the US Navy interested now? You betcha! They nearly bit the hand off the man. They offered him $150,000 for it, named it after him (USS *Holland*) and ordered six more just like it.

If John was hoping the US Navy might use his invention against the British, that didn't work out too well. Instead, the Americans *sold* his plans to Britain so that they could make their own submersibles. HMS *Holland I* became the first submarine in the Royal Navy. Given that he was an Irish-speaking republican (despite falling out with the Fenians) John might not have considered that having a Royal Navy ship called after him was such a huge honour.

PHOTO

NAME JOHN PHILLIP HOLLAND (1841-1914)

OCCUPATION(S) TEACHER, ENGINEER, INVENTOR

UNLIKELY TO SAY:	'We all live in a yellow submarine.'
LIKES:	Fenians
DISLIKES:	Fenians
CLAIM TO FAME:	Inventor of the first submarine to be commissioned by the US Navy

HARRY FERGUSON

The 'mad mechanic' who
developed the tractor.

HENRY GEORGE FERGUSON (better known as Harry) didn't much like working on his father's County Down farm. However, it was probably just as well that he managed to spend a few years employed as an agricultural labourer. Harry left school at the age of 14 but he was a very curious young man and continued his education later in life, becoming a brilliant engineer. Although working on the family farm for his extremely demanding dad denied him a formal early education, it gave him the kind of experience that proved to be very useful later in life when he found his true calling: designing and selling tractors and farm machinery.

But there was a lot more to Harry than tractors and ploughs. His first love was speed (he earned the nickname the 'Mad Mechanic' building and racing motorbikes and cars) and then he moved on to 'heavier than air' flight (that's airplanes to you and me). In 1909, he built an aircraft just by consulting drawings and photographs in a magazine. Then, that New Year's Eve, he became the first person in the UK to build and fly his own plane. The fact that he got it to take off and land without a tragic accident meant that he made it to New Year's Day 1910. However, crashes and narrow escapes came later on, and he was a very lucky man indeed to survive into 1911.

During the First World War, Harry realised that the very basic tractors available in 1914 – imported from the USA – were not up to the task of helping to produce food on the sort of scale necessary to win a war and feed the population of the UK at the same time.

So, he got to work on redesigning the tractor and developing a plough that worked well with his new machine. That was where his experience as a farmhand paid off. He knew exactly what was required: lighter machines that would work better in wet Irish and British conditions.

Just before the Second World War, he did a deal with the famous car maker Henry Ford to produce his tractors in the USA. These two old-fashioned businessmen sealed the deal with a handshake rather than a written contract. This was fine for as long as Henry Ford I was alive, but after he died in 1947, his son, Henry Ford II, pointed out that he hadn't been in on the handshake and that the deal was off. Harry sued Ford Jr for stealing his designs and won his case in 1952, after a long legal battle.

In 1953 Harry's company merged with the giant Canadian agricultural machinery manufacturer Massey-Harris. At first the new company was known as Massey-Harris-Ferguson, but then the name was shortened to the much simpler Massey-Ferguson, a famous brand still familiar today.

Not long after his battle with Henry Ford II, Harry got out of the tractor business, but he wasn't finished with engines. In the 1960s he designed a successful Formula 1 racing car! The 'Mad Mechanic' just did not know when to stop.

PHOTO

NAME HENRY GEORGE 'HARRY' FERGUSON (1884-1960)

OCCUPATION ENGINEER

UNLIKELY TO SAY:	'Vroom, vroom.'
LIKES:	Tinkering with things
DISLIKES:	His strict dad, farming
CLAIM TO FAME:	Adapted the tractor and produced cheap and effective farm machinery

CYNTHIA EVELYN LONGFIELD

She spent her long life chasing dragonflies.

WHILE SHE WAS alive there was probably no one on the planet who knew more about dragonflies than Cynthia Evelyn Longfield. It might be the case that no one has caught up with her to this day.

Cynthia came from a landed Cork family who divided their time between London and a 1,000-acre estate in Munster. Cynthia much preferred Cork because living on a farm allowed her to do what she liked best: roaming around the fields searching for and examining insects. She was also a huge fan of the great 19th-century British scientist Charles Darwin, who came up with the theory of evolution (which, among

other things, established that humans have evolved from apes). In 1924, Cynthia became a member of a scientific expedition that retraced Darwin's travels in the Pacific in the 1830s. This was the journey of the HMS *Beagle* that led to his great work *On the Origin of Species*, which changed the way we look at the world. Cynthia could not be parted from her butterfly net on that trip and she helped collect hundreds of new insect specimens for the Natural History Museum in London.

When she returned from the expedition, Cynthia began to narrow down the scope of her work and decided to concentrate on the study of dragonflies. That may sound like

a really specialist area to which to devote your working life, but there are more than 3,000 species of dragonfly, more than enough research work for a single lifetime. Cynthia also took an interest in other insects on the side, just to make sure no one could accuse her of being obsessed with dragonflies (which, let's face it, she was). Cynthia was known to her colleagues as 'Madam Dragonfly' (if you've ever heard of the opera *Madam Butterfly*, you'll get the joke).

Her fascination with insects took her all over the world. She visited Brazil, Canada, Kenya and South Africa and also travelled right across Europe. She was so fond of Africa that she even bought a coffee farm in Uganda before being driven back to England by the nasty tropical disease malaria.

In 1960 she published her best-known book. It was called *Dragonflies* (I'll bet that came as a shock). After she 'retired' in the late 1950s, she could still be seen wandering around Ireland in a battered old Austin car, carrying binoculars, a walking stick and her moth-eaten butterfly net. A lot of the specimens she captured are to be seen today in the Natural History Museum ('The Dead Zoo') in Dublin.

Even though she lived to the age of 94, chances are that Cynthia still hadn't made the acquaintance of every species of dragonfly before she died. But it wasn't from want of trying.

PHOTO

NAME CYNTHIA EVELYN LONGFIELD (1896-1991)

OCCUPATION NATURALIST

UNLIKELY TO SAY:	'Pesky flies. Where's my repellent?'
LIKES:	Dragonflies
DISLIKES:	Being indoors
CLAIM TO FAME:	One of the most respected entomologists (they study insects) of the 20th century

KATHLEEN LONSDALE

A scientist and a feminist
who worried about the military use
of scientific discoveries.

KATHLEEN YARDLEY WAS born in Newbridge, County Kildare, and you have to wonder just how much she would have been able to achieve as a scientist if her mother hadn't taken her, and her brothers and sisters, to England when she was five years old. If the Yardleys had remained in Newbridge, Kathleen would have been in her twenties in the Ireland of the 1920s. Back then, Ireland was not a good place for a brilliant, adventurous and curious woman to thrive. She had more opportunities in Britain. Thankfully things are far different today.

Kathleen was not from a wealthy background. She was the tenth and youngest child of the Newbridge postmaster, but when her mother took the decision to move the family to England to start a new life, Kathleen won a scholarship to a good English secondary school and was launched on her way to stardom as a scientist. At the age of 19 she so impressed the Nobel Prize-winning physicist W.H. Bragg that he took her on to his team – which was working on X-rays and crystals – at University College, London. One of the other members of the team was Thomas Lonsdale. The two young scientists fell in love and married in 1927. Thomas, recognising his wife's brilliance, encouraged Kathleen to continue her scientific work after they got married.

This was an unusual attitude for a husband to take in the 1920s when women were expected just to work in the home and raise children.

Kathleen continued to do scientific research on crystallography while bringing up three children. In 1936, both she and Thomas became Quakers, members of the religion known formally as the Society of Friends. This was to have a huge impact on her work outside of science as she and her husband became committed pacifists, working for world peace and an end to war. Her opposition to military conflict meant that, during the Second World War, Kathleen was sent to jail for a month for refusing to sign up for war duties. She also opened up her home to refugees from war-torn Europe.

In 1945, Kathleen became the first female professor at University College, London.

She taught chemistry and spent much of her working life, after a late start (she was in her forties before she got a full-time university job), encouraging girls and women to become involved in science. After the Second World War, she grew concerned that scientific research was being used to develop new and more frightening weapons of war. And with good reason: in 1945, the United States dropped the first ever atomic bombs (incredibly destructive weapons) on the Japanese cities of Hiroshima and Nagasaki. They killed hundreds of thousands of people and destroyed both cities.

Kathleen became a leader in the struggle against the spread of nuclear arms and is almost as well-known for fighting for her principles as she was for her breakthrough work as a scientist.

PHOTO

NAME KATHLEEN LONSDALE (NÉE YARDLEY) (1903-1971)

OCCUPATION SCIENTIST

UNLIKELY TO SAY:	'Of course you can use my research to make deadly weapons.'
LIKES:	Crystals
DISLIKES:	Discrimination against women and using science for military purposes
CLAIM TO FAME:	Paved the way for women in science with a number of firsts

JOSEPH MURPHY

The man who invented the most delicious snack known to humanity.

IT'S NOT QUITE as cool as being the first man to walk on the surface of the moon, but the inventor of the flavoured crisp probably means more to most of us than the celebrated American astronaut Neil Armstrong. Moondust or a crisp butty? You decide.

The genius responsible for putting the cheese and the onion into the crisp was one of our own, Joseph Murphy, born in the Liberties in Dublin. If there was a Nobel Prize for savoury snacks, Joe Murphy would have long since been invited to Oslo to receive his gold medal.*

As you would expect, Joe Murphy just had to be nicknamed 'Spud'. All the more so because of the delicious use to which he put the potato. His dad was a builder and his mother owned a paint and wallpaper shop. So nothing there to suggest that Spud was going to make his living in the highly competitive world of savoury snacks.

But above all else, Joe Murphy was a great businessman. At one point in his career he made a living importing Ribena and ball-point pens. (No, I don't see the connection either.) Then he set up a small company called Tayto (you might have heard of them) and got into the crisp business. Dissatisfied with the traditional crisp – they probably reminded him of salted cardboard – he got to work in his kitchen and came up with the far tastier cheese and onion version. That really established the famous Tayto brand, with a lot of help from the father and mother of all neon signs advertising the new product on the corner of Westmoreland Street in Dublin.

Neil Armstrong could probably see it from the surface of the moon when he was collecting all that dust (although he never mentioned it).

Joe Murphy later outdid himself by coming up with the recipe for salt and vinegar and barbecue crisps as well. The man should truly be a saint by now (he died in 2001), but there would probably need to be a pretty hefty petition sent to Rome before the pope would agree to canonise a crisp manufacturer.

The humble Spud (the person, not the vegetable) had no problem showing off his newfound wealth. He drove around Dublin in a posh Rolls-Royce car, which he changed for a new model (always a Rolls-Royce) every year. In 1983, he sold the Tayto company, moved to Spain and spent much of the rest of his life playing golf and sailing.

Forget Walkers. Throw away those chilli tortilla chips. Bury your Carr's Melts in the gap between the cushions of the couch. When it comes to the savoury snack, Tayto is the indisputable Big Cheese (and onion).

*He might not even have been the first Irishman to have such an honour bestowed upon him because his fellow countryman Joseph Haughton invented the cream cracker in 1885.

PHOTO

NAME JOSEPH 'SPUD' MURPHY (1923–2001)

OCCUPATION COOK

UNLIKELY TO SAY:	'Can we get Gary Lineker to promote Tayto?'
LIKES:	Crisps
DISLIKES:	People who call crisps 'chips'
CLAIM TO FAME:	Inventor of the flavoured crisp

PART 5

SLIGHTED SPORTSPERSONS

We Irish love our sport.

Whether we reserve our support and admiration for a distant Premier League soccer club, or a much nearer-at-hand GAA football/hurling county; whether we just like a flutter on the Grand National every year, or can't bear to be parted from the racing pages of the daily newspapers; whether we like to observe others competing from the safety of the living-room couch, or prefer to work up a sweat training for the marathon; whether we are as dedicated as Johnny Sexton or Katie McCabe to one sport and one sport only, or whether we will argue the toss with anyone about any sport under the sun ('I just don't think he had his horse under control in that final chukka'*), we Irish love our sport.

But the chances are you've never heard tell of any of these supreme Irish talents. A gambler, a boxer, a swimmer, a goalkeeper, a tennis player, a fitness fanatic, a pitcher, a camogie player and a golfer. But they are worth reading about … some for all the wrong reasons.

*You will, of course, have identified that our fictional 'expert' was talking about polo – the one on dry land with horses, not the one that requires getting wet.

DENIS O'KELLY

A shrewd professional
gambler who was the scourge
of English bookmakers.

THE EXPRESSION 'UPWARDLY mobile' is one that you will probably hear more and more as you get older. The idea behind it is that a person can be born into poverty and, through their talents, hard work and probably a certain amount of luck, become very successful indeed. The 18th-century prize for being 'upwardly mobile' should go to Irishman Denis O'Kelly.

He was born on a small farm in County Carlow in the mid-1720s. By 1748 he had left Ireland and moved to London. Not that he was much better off there: his first job was as a sedan chair carrier. This meant that he ferried his 'elders and betters' (that's how the people in the chairs saw it anyway) around the streets of the city as they sat above him in splendour.

But Denis had oodles of charm and ambition and it appears that one of the people who liked being transported by him lent him some money so that he could try and improve his lot. This he did by gambling with the money. He managed to do quite well, for a while at least, fleecing his 'elders and betters' until his luck ran out. Then he hit a bad streak, lost everything and ended up in prison because he couldn't pay his gambling debts.

He got out of jail in 1760 and set about getting back on his feet. Second time around, he did not make the same mistakes that had seen him end up in a debtor's prison. He gambled heavily and successfully on horses, and by the end of the decade he ran his own racing stables.

In 1769, Denis made the best investment of his lifetime when he spent £650 – which was a small fortune at the time (about €150,000 today) – on a horse called Eclipse. He wasn't to know it at the time, but he had just won the lottery. Eclipse went on to become the most famous and successful racehorse of the 18th century. Shortly after buying the stallion, Denis made an absolutely outrageous bet. He arrived with his stake money and told the bookmaker that the bet was 'Eclipse first, and the rest nowhere.' This meant he was predicting that his horse would finish an astonishing 240 yards in front of all the other runners in the race. If that proved to be the case, Denis would win his bet. Because it was highly unlikely to happen, he got really good odds. Eclipse duly romped home by more than the required 240 yards (about 200 metres) and Denis made a packet on his hazardous bet.

Denis, because he came from a poor background and spoke with a strong Irish accent (a 'brogue'), was never really accepted by the English upper classes. Despite their disapproval, he took thousands of pounds from them in winning bets and ended his days owning two fine houses, one in Piccadilly in London, the other a country estate in Middlesex. Not bad for a country boy from Carlow.

PHOTO

NAME DENIS O'KELLY
(C. 1725-1787)

OCCUPATION(S) BARMAN,
SEDAN CHAIR CARRIER,
GAMBLER,
RACEHORSE OWNER

DEFINITELY SAID:	'Eclipse first and the rest nowhere.'
LIKES:	Bankrupting rich toffs
DISLIKES:	Losing a bet
CLAIM TO FAME:	Owned the greatest racehorse of the 18th century

PAUL BOYTON

The Dublin showman who became
known as 'The Fearless Frogman'.

DUBLINER PAUL BOYTON, whose family emigrated to Pittsburgh, Pennsylvania in the USA when he was very young, liked water so much that he joined a couple of navies (including the Union Navy in the US Civil War at the age of 15) and loved to mess about in rubber suits. While he spent most of his life as a showman, doing all sorts of aquatic stunts to draw attention to himself, Paul was also one of the founders of something called the United States Life-Saving Service. Today it's better known as the US Coast Guard.

But let's stick with the fun stuff. In the 1870s, Paul adapted a rubber suit that was originally designed to save the lives of steamship passengers. It was like a modern-day wetsuit except that Paul's version also had air pockets to help him float. One of his first stunts was to attempt a crossing of the English Channel in June 1875. He did it in 24 hours, becoming the first man to swim from England to France. However, his exploit is forgotten today because a few months later Captain Matthew Webb accomplished the same feat in 22 hours, without the help of an inflatable suit.

But his Channel crossing was just a paddle in a puddle in comparison with his 1881 trip down the Mississippi river, wearing his trusty inflatable suit and pulling behind him his food for the journey. He began his epic swim near the Canadian border in the state of Montana, engaging the services of *New York Herald* journalist James Creelman to publicise the event. Paul floated down the river for 1,675 miles, spending 64 days in the water; Creelman moved ahead of him on land, informed the locals of the next downriver

town and made sure that 'The Fearless Frogman' had many welcoming committees waiting for him along the way. The object of the exercise was to sell rubber suits.

A few years after that wild journey, Paul put his talents as a showman to good use when he joined the famous circus owned by P.T. Barnum (have you seen the film *The Greatest Showman*? Good. Then you know who P.T. Barnum is). Later he opened his own water-based amusement park in Chicago, called Paul Boyton's Water Chutes. A few years later he opened Sea Lion Park on Coney Island in New York, fencing in 16 acres of land and charging admission. Paul even got in on the movie business. In 1900, he made

a short silent film that featured him feeding his money-making sea lions. It has the highly imaginative title *Feeding Sea Lions*.

In 1993, almost 70 years after his death, Paul was admitted to the International Swimming Hall of Fame, where he joined people like Johnny Weissmuller, the Olympic swimmer who first played Tarzan, and Hollywood actress Esther Williams, who appeared in a lot of what became known as 'aquamusicals' (plenty of water and singing).

So, although he never quite learned how to walk on water, he still became very famous, just as long as he was wet.

PHOTO

NAME PAUL BOYTON
(1848-1924)

OCCUPATION(S) SHOWMAN,
STUNTMAN,
OPEN WATER SWIMMER

UNLIKELY TO SAY:	'Glug, glug … help!'
LIKES:	Water and rubber suits
DISLIKES:	Jellyfish
CLAIM TO FAME:	First man to swim the English Channel and float down the Mississippi

WILLIAM McCRUM

The Armagh goalkeeper who invented the penalty kick.

THE MAN WHO came up with the idea of the penalty kick in soccer was Irish. He was also a goalkeeper. Which of those two statements sounds more incredible?

Obviously not the first one – I mean, why wouldn't an Irishman come up with such an idea? But a goalkeeper? Come on. Penalty kicks are the bane of a goalkeeper's life: 'Do I dive to the left? Do I dive to the right? If I dive one way or the other will he just hit it down the middle and make me look like a right eejit? What am I going to ... Oh, too late, he's taken it – just give me a few seconds to pick the ball out of the back of the net.'

William McCrum was from Milford in County Armagh, the centre of the linen trade in

Ireland. That's where his family made its money. Money that he managed to lose when he took over the business. An indication as to why that was might be clear from a trip he made in his youth to Monte Carlo. In that fun city's famous casino, over a single weekend, his losses amounted to six figures. That's six figures to the left of the decimal point! But, we're not here to discuss what a lousy businessman and gambler he was. Or to learn about decimals.

William was also a sportsman. He played cricket, rugby and soccer. But we're not here to discuss his prowess at cricket, or at rugby either (not great), we're here to ask why a soccer goalkeeper would have a rush of blood to the head and suggest that members of the opposing team should be able to place the ball on a small spot 11 metres from

the goal line and get a free kick with only the goalkeeper to beat.

The answer to that question lies in William's sense of fair play. For years he had watched as defenders brought down forwards in the penalty area, or handled the ball as it was about to cross the goal line, with no consequence other than a free kick. The defending team was then allowed to bring all its players behind the ball. So whoever was taking the free kick was going to have a hard time finding a way through that mob. William suggested the idea of the penalty kick to the governing body of Irish soccer. They, in turn, brought it to the International Football Association Board, which has

looked after the rules of the game since 1886. Not everyone was immediately taken by William's idea, but it eventually found its way into the rule book in 1891. So, anyone who fails to score in a penalty shootout has William McCrum to blame for his or her embarrassment.

By the way, William wasn't a great goalkeeper. He played for Milford in the Irish Football League and in the 1890/91 season they lost all 14 of their games. Poor William had to pick the ball out of the back of the net 62 times.

At least none of them were penalties!

PHOTO

NAME WILLIAM MCCRUM
(1865-1932)

OCCUPATION(S) LINEN MANUFACTURER, SOCCER GOALKEEPER

LIKELY TO SAY:	'Offside, ref.'
LIKES:	Fair play, gambling
DISLIKES:	Conceding goals, losing money in casinos
CLAIM TO FAME:	Devised the penalty kick in soccer

JOHN PIUS BOLAND

The Irish winner of the
first Olympic tennis singles
and doubles championships.

HIS FULL NAME was John Mary Pius Boland (you would be surprised at how many Irish males used to have a Mary somewhere in their names) and he came from a wealthy background. He was the son of a member of the Boland family firm (whose Dublin factories produced flour, bread and biscuits for decades until it merged with its main competitor, Jacob's, in the 1970s). John went to London and Oxford universities and became a barrister in 1897. He was also a keen member of the Gaelic League, although he never quite mastered the Irish language.

But it was a pretty random event in 1896 that changed his life. Although he went on to become a member of parliament for almost 20 years, it is for his talent with a tennis racket that he is celebrated. He happened to be on holiday in Greece when the first modern Olympic Games took place in Athens (where the ancient Olympics had ended around AD 400). A friend of his was on the organising committee of the Games and suggested to John, who was a multi-talented athlete, that it would be a lark if he were to compete. He suggested John try the tennis tournament, as he was handy with a racket (or 'racquet' if you prefer). John hadn't packed any tennis gear before travelling to Greece, so he had to improvise (make it up as he went along). He bought a second-hand racket in a street market, but he couldn't manage to secure a pair of tennis shoes at short notice, so he just played in his street shoes. It didn't affect his performance, however. He won the men's singles titles, as well as sharing in the men's doubles title.

This would have made him the first Irish gold medallist at an Olympic Games, except that, technically, he didn't win an actual gold medal. First prize back then was a diploma congratulating him on being an Olympic champion, a silver medal and a sort of tiara made of olive branches to wear on his head just in case he didn't want to wave his diploma around to remind everybody that he was an Olympic champion.

One Olympic tradition that remains to this day, however, was the raising of the national flag as the winner was awarded his (all the 1896 participants were male) prize. That presented the organising committee with a problem. Although John was Irish, he was, officially at least, competing as a citizen of the United Kingdom. Ireland was not allowed to send athletes under the green, white and orange tricolour until after we won our independence in 1922. When John was told that the Union Jack would be raised as he was being handed his diploma, silver medal and olive branch crown, he wasn't having any of it. He insisted on an Irish flag and he got his way.

Ten years later, in 1906, Irish athletics gold medallist Peter O'Connor would be forced to climb the flagpole, tear down the Union Jack and replace it with an Irish flag (a golden harp and shamrock on a green background) at his own presentation ceremony. So, John Pius Boland had it easy.

PHOTO

NAME JOHN PIUS BOLAND
(1870-1958)

OCCUPATION(S) POLITICIAN,
LAWYER,
TENNIS PLAYER

LIKELY TO SAY:	'Aced that one.'
LIKES:	Tennis, the Irish language
DISLIKES:	The fact that he never quite mastered Irish
CLAIM TO FAME:	Winner of two 'gold medals' at the Athens Olympics of 1896

MARY BAGOT STACK

Founder of an international women's health and fitness movement.

IN MANY WAYS, Mary Bagot Stack (better known as 'Molly') did not have an awful lot of good luck. She suffered from illness as a child; her first marriage failed; her second husband died in the early days of the First World War; and she developed cancer in her forties that led to her death at the age of just 51. However, she made the world a far better place for others. She changed the lives of thousands of women, and founded a worldwide organisation that exists to this day.

Molly was born in Dublin. As a child she suffered from rheumatic fever (which causes painful joints and can lead to heart problems), so she began to do fitness and body-building exercises at an early age in order to help her recovery. Fitness became very important to both her physical and her mental health. She wanted to pass on to other women what she had learned in her own youth. So, she began to organise fitness and movement classes for female factory workers in the 1920s.

In 1909, Molly married a Dublin medical student named Albert McCreery. She quickly realised that she had made a mistake and that she was not in love with him. As you might expect, after a start like that, the marriage didn't work. She divorced Albert, having never actually lived with him, and then, in 1912, married her third cousin, an army officer named Hugh Bagot Stack. This meant that she got her original name back. The newly married couple lived in India, where Hugh was stationed with his regiment. They had a daughter (Prunella) together. Sadly, that marriage did not last long either. When the First World War broke out,

Hugh was sent to France and was killed in November 1914.

Molly's interest in physical fitness for women led her to found the Women's League of Health and Beauty in 1930. Her methods were based on some of the exercises she had used as a child, as well as a number of yoga moves she had learned from her life in India. The League was an instant success and eventually made Molly famous worldwide. Her book *Building the Body Beautiful*, published in 1931, became a sort of bible for the many thousands of members of the organisation. She called her method 'The Bagot Stack Stretch and Swing System', which, on the face of it, sounds a lot like a form of torture or execution. But 170,000 women can't be wrong, and that was how many members the Women's League of Health and Beauty could boast by 1940.

Molly's league survives today as the Fitness League, and the 'Stretch and Swing System' has become the 'flexercise' method. After Molly died in 1935, her daughter Prunella kept the flag flying for the Bagot Stack family and continued her mother's work. Prunella herself lived to the ripe old age of 96!

PHOTO

NAME MARY 'MOLLY' BAGOT STACK (1883–1935)

OCCUPATION HEALTH AND FITNESS GURU

UNLIKELY TO SAY:	'Go on, have that cream bun.'
LIKES:	Stretching
DISLIKES:	Sitting still
CLAIM TO FAME:	Founder of the Women's League of Health and Beauty

JOE CLEARY

Officially the worst pitcher
ever to play professional baseball.

IF YOU'VE EVER watched American sports on TV, you'll know that they just love their statistics. 'Stats' are the figures used to measure the performances of athletes: how far or how fast they throw a ball; how speedy they are; how much weight they can lift. The sport of baseball has been keeping these measurements for decades. A Corkman named Joe Cleary probably wished they hadn't started until *after* he had pitched in his only appearance in the 'Major Leagues' (the highest level of the professional game). Joe's family left Ireland for New York in 1928, when he was ten years old, so he learned to play baseball in his teens. His nickname was 'Fire' because he could throw a baseball hard and fast.

Joe was a pitcher for the Washington Senators Major League team. A pitcher is a bit like a bowler in cricket (or a pitcher in rounders). His job is to throw the ball towards a batter on the opposing team. If he gets the ball past the batter three times (those are called strikes), then the batter is out. If the batter manages to hit the ball, and it isn't quickly intercepted or caught while in the air, then he can move to the next base and another batter comes up to try his luck.

Luck was in short supply for Joe on 4 August 1945 when he was brought on as a substitute pitcher in his first Major League game, which was against the Boston Red Sox. It was the first game in which his personal statistics would be recorded. All he had to do was to get three batters out and he could go back to the dugout at the end of the 'inning' to the praise of his manager and teammates.

It all started well, with Joe managing to get the first batter out. Unfortunately for Joe, retiring (getting out) that single batter was as good as it got. He came up short against the next eight batters and gave up seven runs to the Red Sox.

In baseball, a pitcher's entire career is measured by something called his 'earned run average' (ERA), a figure that is calculated using the number of runs the pitcher allows the other team to score. Joe never pitched for any Major League team again, so his career ERA of 189.00 was based on the balls that he threw at that one Washington Senators/Red Sox game. Now 189.00 may sound OK, but an ERA is like a golf score: the lower the better. Joe's is the worst ever recorded by a pitcher in more than a century of baseball statistics. The best ever career ERA by a pitcher is 1.82 – more than a hundred times better than poor 'Fire' Cleary's effort.

He must have been hoping that someone would holler his nickname from the stands and everyone would race to the exits. After giving up seven runs, his manager decided to take him out of the game. As if giving up seven runs wasn't bad enough for poor Joe, he was replaced by a pitcher who had lost a leg while serving in the Second World War.

You just couldn't make this stuff up.

PHOTO

NAME JOE 'FIRE' CLEARY
(1918-2004)

OCCUPATION PROFESSIONAL
BASEBALL PLAYER

UNLIKELY TO SAY:	'Yes! Strike three.'
LIKES:	Throwing baseballs at top speed
DISLIKES:	Watching those baseballs being hit out of the ground
CLAIM TO FAME:	Statistically, the worst pitcher in professional baseball

KAY MILLS

The starriest of stars
in the world of camogie.

HOW WELL DO you know your Gaelic games? Try this piece of trivia: which player has won the most All-Ireland championship medals in a single GAA field sport?*

'King' Henry Shefflin of Kilkenny? Good guess – he is out on his own with 10 hurling championship medals. Páidí Ó Sé of Kerry? Close, but no cream bun – he has won 8 football medals, a record he shares with 11 other players. Rena Buckley or Briege Corkery? Even closer, but still no chocolate fudge cake. They have won 18 All-Irelands each – but they are both dual players who have 11 football and 7 camogie All-Ireland winners medals on their mantelpieces.

Give up? You've probably never heard of her.

The answer is Kathleen 'Kay' Mills, who first appeared for Dublin in the All-Ireland Camogie final in 1941, four days after her 18th birthday. She ended up with a disappointing runners-up medal that day, as Cork won their third All-Ireland title in a row. It was a tough start for young Mills as it was a real grudge match, with fights between players breaking out all over the pitch. But Kay made up for it the following year when Dublin beat Cork in the 1942 final, after a replay. She then went on to win a phenomenal 15 All-Ireland senior medals in 17 appearances over a career that lasted 20 years.

Kay was born in Inchicore just as the Irish Civil War was coming to an end. She took up camogie at the age of five. Because her dad was a railway worker, she was able to join the Great Southern Railway sports club.

Her father had two pence a week deducted from his wages for membership of the club. Well worth it, given what Kay accomplished.

Winning three O'Duffy Cups (the trophy awarded to the All-Ireland Camogie Championship winners every year) in a row between 1942 and 1944 was quite an achievement for Dublin, but that was nothing in comparison with their form between 1950 and 1955. The Dubs were just unbeatable and won six All-Irelands in a row, with Kay playing on each of the teams. Oddly, despite being the most experienced player in the side through most of the 1950s,

Kathy only collected the O'Duffy Cup in person once, as team captain in 1958.

She won her last medal in 1961, on her 38th birthday. It was her final appearance for the Dublin senior team. Today, the winners of the All-Ireland Junior Camogie Championship each year carry off ... the Kay Mills Cup.

*You might have noticed that I have cleverly excluded handball, which is not a 'field' sport!

PHOTO

NAME KATHLEEN 'KAY' ROSALEEN MILLS (1923-1996)

OCCUPATION SPORTING SUPERSTAR

LIKES:	Medals
DISLIKES:	Cork
CLAIM TO FAME:	Winner of 15 All-Ireland senior camogie medals

PHILOMENA GARVEY

She blazed a trail for Irish
women golfers for three decades.

THESE DAYS WE are used to Irish golfing glory in major international championships, but that was not always the case, especially in the women's game. In the middle of the 20th century, years before American golf fans began to chant 'USA! USA!' at Ryder Cup matches, or 'You de maaaaan!' at the US Masters, we only had one female standard bearer in golf: Philomena Garvey. After dominating the amateur game for almost 20 years, she became Ireland's first female professional. For a long time, she was our *only* female professional golfer.

It helped that Philomena was born in the County Louth village of Baltray, within driving distance (we're talking golf clubs, not cars here) of one of the best courses in Ireland, the County Louth Golf Club (better known as Baltray). It is what's known as a 'links' course, meaning it was built into the sand dunes of the seaside, and when the wind blows there it is capable of cutting you in half and blowing your body out to sea (that's only a slight exaggeration). If you can hit a golf ball into the wind on a course like that, then you can hit it anywhere.

And boy, could Philomena Garvey hit a golf ball! She won her first Irish championship in 1946 at the age of 20. The following year she was asked to choose between marriage and golf. The fact that she won another 14 Irish championships should offer a clue as to the decision she made. She also worked in Clerys department store on O'Connell Street, selling golf clubs, shoes and carts, but the owners gave her plenty of opportunities to pursue her first love, playing golf.

Every two years, Britain and Ireland compete against the USA in an event called the Curtis Cup. This pits the best British and Irish amateur women golfers against the best Americans. Philomena played in the Curtis Cup six times. It should have been seven, but in 1958, although she had been selected to play, she withdrew from the team. She had a major problem with the team sweaters that the British and Irish team were being given to wear. The only emblem was the Union Jack, and she wasn't going to put up with that. Two years later she was chosen again. This time she played in the event, as the sweaters had been changed to recognise that there was an Irish golfer on the team.

In 1964, Philomena turned professional. She gave it her best for a few years but playing for money didn't work out for her, and in 1968 she applied to become an amateur again. Two years after being allowed back into amateur competitions, she won her last Irish championship. She retired from competitive golf shortly afterwards.

Her death at the age of 83 was probably as she would have wanted it – she died as she was passing through the entrance of Baltray clubhouse. A golfer to the end.

PHOTO

NAME PHILOMENA GARVEY
(1926-2009)

OCCUPATION GOLFER

UNLIKELY TO:	Cough loudly when an opponent was putting
LIKES:	Birdies and eagles
DISLIKES:	Bogies and double bogies
CLAIM TO FAME:	Ireland's leading female golfer for three decades

PART 6

OVERLOOKED ADVENTURERS

It's hard to define what an adventurer is, except by saying that you'd know one if you saw one. They are the kind of people who climb mountains or explore wildernesses where no one has ever been before. They step well outside their 'comfort zone' (that's the area in front of the couch in the sitting room, between the sofa and the telly) and do things that most of us would find pretty scary. Ireland boasts hundreds of these people with serious cases of 'ants in their pants' whose idea of adventure goes a bit beyond trying out for the local football team or auditioning for a part in a play (both of which, in fairness, also require quite a lot of courage). Welcome to the stories of, among others, the first woman to become a judge in India, two Cavanmen who changed the American west and one who didn't, and the Galwayman who brought camels to Australia but didn't live to tell the tale.

DEAN MAHOMET

The Indian adventurer who became a part of 18th-century Cork society.

WE IRISH LIKE to think of ourselves as being against 'empire'. This probably stems from the time we spent as a reluctant part of the British version. So we don't like to be reminded of the enthusiastic role Irish men (and one or two women) played in the creation of that empire. Ireland provided many of the soldiers who either won, or guarded, British colonies, as well as a lot of the civil servants who governed places like India.

So it is interesting to record an adventurer who travelled in the opposite direction. He came from India and settled in Cork for 25 years. His name was Dean Mahomet and, among other things, he is said to have introduced Indian food to Europe. Anyone who has ever eaten in one of Ireland's many fabulous Indian restaurants has umpteen

delicious reasons to be grateful to Dean if that is indeed the case.

Dean came from a Muslim family. When he was around 11 years old, his father, who served on behalf of Britain in the Indian army, died in battle. Dean was then taken under the wing of an Irish-born Indian army officer, Captain Godfrey Evan Baker, who was from a wealthy Cork family and who became a sort of 'second father' to him. When Godfrey returned to Ireland in 1784, Dean went with him. There, although he was in his twenties, Dean went back to school to improve his English. He also fell in love with a Corkwoman, Jane Daly. Her family did not want the couple to marry so, in 1786, they eloped and got hitched without the permission of the Daly family. The other people of Cork didn't seem to mind. Dean was largely accepted into Cork society,

although his relationship with the wealthy Baker family would have played a part in that.

Two other major events occurred in the life of Dean Mohamet in 1786: he converted from Islam to Christianity, and his patron, Godfrey, died. Some years later, Godfrey's brother, Captain William Massey Baker, returned from India. He bought an estate near Cork on which Dean and Jane were allowed to live.

In 1793, Dean showed how well-liked he was in Cork society when he succeeded in getting more than 300 people to subscribe to the publication of a book entitled *The Travels of Dean Mohamet*, which introduced India to a Munster audience. It was a bit like a Kickstarter campaign – everyone who subscribed got a copy.

Then, rather suddenly, although he was settled in Cork and approaching his fifties, Dean decided to emigrate to London in 1807. The move may have been connected to the marriage of William Massey Baker to Mary Towgood Davies the same year. The new 'lady of the manor' may have disapproved of the presence of Dean and Jane near her new home.

Sadly, from then on, when Dean Mohamet discussed his life (which ended in his nineties!), he wrote Cork out of his story. From 1807 onwards he would always claim that, in 1784, he had travelled directly from India to London.

PHOTO

NAME SAKE DEAN MAHOMET
(1759–1851)
....
OCCUPATION BUSINESSMAN

UNLIKELY TO SAY:	'Up the Rebel county.'
LIKES:	Godfrey Evan Baker
DISLIKES:	Mary Towgood Davies
CLAIM TO FAME:	A reverse adventurer who came from India to Ireland

BUCK WHALEY

Known as 'Jerusalem' Whaley
because of one wild journey to
the Holy Land ... for a bet!

THOMAS WHALEY WAS a rake. Not one of the rakes that you buy in a hardware store which leap up and hit you in the eye if you step on their teeth. A rake is also someone who drinks and gambles a lot and generally behaves very badly. This costs a lot of money and is best left to the rich. Another word for a 'rake' in the 1700s was a 'buck'. That is how Thomas 'Buck' Whaley got his nickname. He once rode a horse out of a third-floor window and broke his leg. Buck broke his leg, that is, not the horse. The poor animal didn't survive the fall.

Whaley and his unlovable father, Richard Chapell Whaley (who used to burn down Catholic churches as a hobby), were both members of the Hellfire Club, a group of rich men who liked to dare each other to do outrageous stunts. This was how 'Buck' got his other nickname, 'Jerusalem'. The fabulously wealthy Duke of Leinster challenged Buck to make the extremely dangerous journey from Dublin to the Holy Land and return with proof that he had visited Jerusalem. The duke would give Buck a colossal £15,000 (that would be more than £2 million today) if he could do it; Buck would give the duke the same if he could not. The duke could well afford it, and what did Buck have to lose? If he didn't make it back to Dublin, it was probably because he had been killed along the way and wouldn't have to pay the money anyway. He set off in October 1788 and was back, with proof, by the following summer. The £15,000 probably didn't last him very long, though: Buck

Whaley went through money like a red-hot poker through a packet of marshmallows.

Two years after he earned the nickname 'Jerusalem', his gambling debts meant that it wasn't safe to remain in Ireland any longer (too many people were looking for him because he owed them money) so he left the country for the Isle of Man. While there he took up another interesting challenge: to live on Irish soil while he was outside of Ireland. In order to win, he brought in shiploads of Irish earth and built a house on it!

Buck died young – he was only 34. It's reckoned that he went through a fortune of around £400,000 in his short lifetime. That's £400,000 in 18th-century money, which would be millions of euros today!

For a long time his name was kept alive in the nightclub Buck Whaley's in Dublin (it closed down in 2015) where lots of respectable people gathered in the evenings, didn't gamble, had a few drinks and didn't ride horses from the top floor of the building. Most of them anyway.

PHOTO

NAME THOMAS 'BUCK' WHALEY, AKA 'JERUSALEM' WHALEY (1766–1800)

OCCUPATION RAKE (THAT'S SOMEONE WHO MISBEHAVES AND SPENDS LOTS OF MONEY)

LIKES:	Drinking and gambling
DISLIKES:	Working for a living
CLAIM TO FAME:	Going through a fortune in a lifetime of gambling and drinking (don't try this at home!)

THOMAS FITZPATRICK

Known as 'Broken Hand', he was one of the greatest pioneers of the American west.

THOMAS FITZPATRICK IS one of those people who is far better known in America than in his native country. He emigrated from County Cavan to the USA in his late teens. There he was nicknamed 'Broken Hand' by the Native American tribes of the American west after coming off second best in an encounter with his own rifle.

In 1823 he answered an advertisement that was to change his life. It was a call for 'fur trappers' – men who hunted beavers for their skins in the north-west of the country.

Thomas took up the challenge and went on to become one of the most famous 'mountain men' (another name for fur trappers) in American history. He led the first expedition of white men to discover the famous South Pass – a route through the Rocky Mountains that sloped upwards gently enough to allow wagons to pass with ease – and he survived many encounters with hostile Native American tribes (on whose land, let's face it, he was trespassing). Though he came off worse in one confrontation with members of the Gros Ventre nation and was forced to abandon his horse, take to his feet and live off the land for almost a fortnight, while also hiding from the Gros Ventre, who were determined to catch and kill him. Thomas survived the ordeal, but by the end of it, his hair had turned white!

His 'discovery' of South Pass (Native Americans had been using it for centuries) proved useful when the fur trade died out in the 1840s, as Thomas became one of the most sought-after guides to the area.

He led wagons of migrants across the Rocky Mountains, people who were looking to take up good agricultural land in the states of California and Oregon. Later he guided the famous explorer John C. Fremont when he was given the task of mapping much of the American west.

Thomas's final and most important job was to keep the peace in the American west, working as what the government called an 'Indian agent'. This meant that he was a sort of ambassador of the US government in Washington to nations like the Lakota, Cheyenne, Crow and many others. He was greatly respected by many Native American tribes (though maybe not the Gros Ventre so much!), and in 1851 he persuaded a number of them to sign the Treaty of Fort Laramie. This offered guarantees of land in return for keeping the peace and allowing migrants to cross their territory to California.

The peace lasted until shortly after Thomas died (in Washington DC) in 1854. The US government, as it did with so many such treaties, went back on its word and cheated the Native Americans, taking their better land and forcing them on to poor-quality areas known as 'reservations'. Without Thomas's presence, the peace was quickly shattered and the 'Wild West' was in an almost constant state of war for decades.

PHOTO

NAME THOMAS FITZPATRICK
(1799-1854)

OCCUPATION(S) TRAPPER,
GUIDE,
ARMY SCOUT,
INDIAN AGENT

LIKELY TO SAY:	'It's OK. I know a shortcut.'
LIKES:	The open air
DISLIKES:	Much of the Gros Ventre nation
CLAIM TO FAME:	As a fur trapper, helped to open up the American west

JAMES O'CONNELL

Tall tales and tantalising tattoos from an adventurous Irishman.

A CENTURY AND A half before *Riverdance* won the hearts of the American public, another Irish performer was knocking their socks off with the story of how his Irish dancing skills had saved his life. But that wasn't the only thing that grabbed their attention about James O'Connell. Just as interesting was his body, because he was adorned from head to foot in strange and exotic tattoos. Nowadays many people sport tattoos, but back in the 1830s, they tended to be seen only on sailors and convicted prisoners. When James became a star in P.T. Barnum's circus (remember him? *The Greatest Showman*?), not only did O'Connell have more tattoos per square centimetre than the singer-songwriter Ed Sheeran but he also had a fascinating story about how he had come by his body art.

James was from the Liberties in Dublin and, at an early age, became a sailor. That much we can be sure of. The rest ... well, decide for yourselves. In his life story, written in 1836, he claimed that he had been shipwrecked in the southern Pacific and washed up in 1829 on the small island of Pohnpei. There the natives couldn't quite make up their minds how to kill this unwelcome stranger, until he began to dance an Irish jig. That, he claimed afterwards, was what saved his life. They were so impressed with Irish dancing that, instead of doing away with him, the Pohnpeians decided to marry him off to the king's daughter. In preparation for the wedding, they covered his body in elaborate tattoos. That involved a week of intense pain for poor James, who must have wondered if he would have been better off to have let the Pohnpeians kill him straightaway.

James lived on Pohnpei for five years before he was able to make his escape. He arrived in the USA in the 1830s and made his living by joining P.T. Barnum and telling his story, while showing off his tattoos, to goggling audiences all across America. As an encore, he would also show off his Irish dancing skills to the American punters – the same skills that he claimed had saved his life on Pohnpei.

While most of his audience believed his story, on the basis that reality is often stranger than fiction, there were also a lot of people who thought O'Connell was a liar and a chancer (being American they would have called him a 'grifter' or a 'conman'). Whether or not his tall tale was true, one other thing *is* certain: in the mid-19th century, tattoos began to become popular. This might have had nothing whatever to do with James F. O'Connell and P.T. Barnum but you never know …

PHOTO

NAME JAMES F. O'CONNELL (1808-1854)

OCCUPATION CIRCUS PERFORMER

UNLIKELY TO SAY:	'I think I still have a wee bit of room for an I Love Mum on my big toe.'
LIKES:	Tattoos
DISLIKES:	Being stuck on a small Pacific island
CLAIM TO FAME:	Said to have popularised tattoos in the USA

ROBERT O'HARA BURKE

He crossed Australia
from south to north, but
didn't make it back.

DID YOU KNOW that three of the four men who made the first successful south-to-north journey across Australia (from the city of Melbourne to the Gulf of Carpentaria on the north coast) were Irish? It's true! Though sadly they spent a tad too much time wandering about in the sun, and only one of them made it home.

The leader of that ill-fated expedition was Robert O'Hara Burke from Loughrea, County Galway. In 1853, after a stint as a soldier and a spell as a policeman based in Phoenix Park in Dublin, he emigrated to Australia. There, he worked for a while as a policeman. In 1860, the government of the state of Victoria decided to organise an expedition to see if it was possible for human beings to survive the intense heat of the central desert region of the country, and make it all the way to the north coast. Robert asked to be allowed to lead the expedition and his request was granted. In August 1860, he headed off with 17 men, 23 horses and two years' supply of food. Oh yes, and he also took 25 camels! They were not exactly native to Australia but as they are renowned for their ability to survive in high temperatures without a drop of water to wet their lips, someone thought it might be a good idea. In the end, it wasn't the camels who messed up – it was the humans.

Robert became unhappy with the slow progress of the expedition and decided he could move more quickly with a smaller group. He managed to make the north coast with three companions – Englishman William Wills and two fellow Irishmen, John King and Charles Gray – however, weakened by hunger (the four men had not brought enough food) and suffering from exposure to the melting sun, only John King made it back. He'd managed to survive because he'd been taken in by a group of Aboriginal people (native Australians) who knew their way around the desert far better than Europeans. They fed, nursed and kept him alive.

Robert O'Hara Burke died of starvation and exhaustion on 28 June 1861. He was buried where he died, but his body was later dug up and brought back to Melbourne, where he was given a state funeral. A statue of Robert and of William Wills was erected in the middle of Victoria's capital city.

And what about the camels, I hear you ask? To this day, travellers in the remotest regions of the furnace-like interior of Australia often come across these strangely out-of-place animals wandering in the desert. They are probably not looking for poor Robert O'Hara Burke, but are the descendants of his original 25-strong camel company.

PHOTO

NAME ROBERT O'HARA BURKE (1821–1861)

OCCUPATION(S) SOLDIER, POLICEMAN, EXPLORER

LIKELY TO SAY:	'Why don't we try camels?'
LIKES:	Exploring
DISLIKES:	Desert heat
CLAIM TO FAME:	Leader of an (ill-fated) expedition to cross the continent of Australia

MARCUS DALY

The fabulously wealthy
'Copper King' of Butte, Montana.

MARCUS DALY BADLY wanted to make his fortune from mining silver. Sadly, he had to be content with making millions of dollars from copper instead. As they might say in his native county of Cavan, ''twas bad about him', which basically means he had nothing to complain about. And indeed, he didn't do much complaining, unless it was about his great rival, William Clark.

Marcus, the youngest of 11 children, emigrated to the USA at the age of 15. He had no particular skills, little education, and worked as a manual labourer in New York until he had saved enough money to travel west and move in with a sister who had already settled in California. It was the 1860s, and lots of adventurers were feverishly trying to find silver in neighbouring Nevada.

Marcus wanted to try his luck. He became a miner in 1871, and within 10 years he had made enough money to buy an old silver mine, the Anaconda, near the town of Butte, Montana. He reckoned there was enough silver left in the mine to make a living. What he hadn't expected was his huge stroke of luck when enormous deposits of copper were discovered in his mine. Copper was starting to be used a lot in industry, especially in the making of copper wire. Within a few years, the Anaconda was turning out millions of dollars worth of copper every year.

What was a simple boy from Cavan going to do with all that money? He was going to enjoy it, that's what. He built himself a huge mansion (just for the summer – not even all the year round) near Butte. When it was finished, he thought it looked too much

like a church and had it redone! He bought racehorses, and the jockeys wore the colours copper and green. (Get it? Of course you do.) He liked one of his horses, Tammany, so much that he built him a castle. As you would.

One person he really didn't like was fellow mine owner William Clark. When Clark ran for one of the two Montana seats in the United States Senate, Marcus did what he could to make him lose, preferably as humiliatingly as possible. Lots of money changed hands to buy people's votes and make sure that Clark never got near the Senate seat.

William Clark, however, beat Marcus in another of their very personal battles.

There was to be a vote on which town would become the state capital of Montana. Marcus had built a town, also called Anaconda, around his mine, and he wanted it to win; Clark wanted the town of Helena to win. Lots more money changed hands but Clark must have outspent Marcus. Helena finished 2,000 votes ahead of Anaconda and became the state capital.

Marcus Daly died of a heart attack in 1900 at the age of 58. Four decades after he'd arrived in New York as a penniless teenager, he left property worth $75 million. The following year, in 1901, William Clark became ... Senator William Clark! Marcus is still turning in his grave.

PHOTO

NAME MARCUS DALY
(1841–1900)

OCCUPATION(S) MINE OWNER,
'COPPER KING'

UNLIKELY TO SAY:	'You win, Senator Clark.'
LIKES:	Copper
DISLIKES:	William Clark
CLAIM TO FAME:	Millionaire owner of the Anaconda copper mine

MICHAEL MEAGHER

The Irish lawman who lived
by the gun and died
by the gun.

N THE 1870s, after a huge railroad was built across America connecting the eastern cities to California, someone got the bright idea of using trains to move cattle from states like Texas to places like Chicago and Philadelphia, where they would fetch far better prices. As a result, small 'cow towns' (like Wichita and Abilene in Kansas) grew up around the railway stations in the middle of America to which the cattle were being moved. Guiding the cattle along the trails from Texas were some pretty wild and daring cowboys. When they got to the cow towns, things could get lively and very violent, as all the cowboys carried guns. So, these new towns needed policemen/law enforcement officers who were as handy with their guns as the cowboys.

That is how Michael Meagher, born in Cavan in 1843, was appointed as town marshal of Wichita in 1871. He knew his way around firearms. However, he was reluctant to use them and developed a reputation for being able to defuse tense and dangerous situations with rowdy cowboys without having to fire his gun. He insisted that everyone hand over their weapons before they were let into any town where he was sheriff.

However, he was finally forced to use his weapon, with deadly effect, in 1877. He was sitting on the outside loo of a bar/saloon in Wichita (true story!) when someone fired at him and missed. Quickly pulling up his pants, he chased after the gunman and cornered him.

Rather than wait to be fired at again, Michael took aim and killed the man.

Despite being a law enforcement officer, Michael was no saint. In the olden days (*well* before your parents were kids!) it wasn't always clear who were the good guys and who were the bad guys when it came to maintaining law and order. This was especially true in the American 'Wild West'. You might be a bank robber in one state, with wanted posters offering large amounts of money for your capture, 'DEAD or ALIVE!'. But if you crossed into a neighbouring state, you might be able to get a job as a lawman. In fact, if you were sneaky enough, you might even be able to do both at the same time!

In 1880, Michael moved to the growing town of Caldwell, Kansas where he was elected mayor. However, to make a bit of money on the side, he also ran an illegal gambling operation, for which he was fined when he was caught. That didn't stop him from becoming town marshal the following year. It was to be his last job. On 17 December 1881, Michael chased down a cowboy named Talbot who was making a nuisance of himself. Talbot was cornered but was quicker on the draw and Michael was shot. As he lay dying, Michael called out, 'Tell my wife I have got it at last.' Talbot escaped, but was gunned down in California a few years later.

In the 'Wild West' if you lived by the gun, you tended to die by the gun.

PHOTO

NAME MICHAEL MEAGHER
(1843-1881)

OCCUPATION(S) GUNFIGHTER,
LAWMAN

UNLIKELY TO SAY:	'Reach for the sky, *hombre*.'
LIKES:	Law and order
DISLIKES:	Cowboys
CLAIM TO FAME:	One of the best lawmen in the American West

ALBERT CASHIER

The Irishwoman who became an
Irishman and joined the Union army.

IN THE MID-19TH century, society had certain expectations about what it meant to be male or female. Men went to war; women stayed at home and worried about whether their husbands, sons or brothers would ever come back. A woman might have preferred to live life as a man – and there were many reasons that might be the case, not least the lower status of women in society, but because of those expectations, people tended to stick to the gender assigned to them at birth.

Not Jennie Hodgers, however. She was from Clogherhead in County Louth and her first big adventure involved getting out of Ireland at the age of 16. She stowed away on board a boat to England and eventually made her way to the USA. She settled in the state of Illinois in the middle of the country, but when the American Civil War broke out, she made a life-altering decision. No matter what it took, she was going to join the Union army (forces loyal to the elected US president, Abraham Lincoln) and take part in the fight against slavery. There was only one practical obstacle: the army didn't recruit women. Whether Jennie was transgender and identified as male, was an adventurous type and wanted to go to war, or was attracted by the prospect of getting three meals a day, $13 a month and a pension (if she survived), we will never know, but in 1862, when she was 19 years old, Jennie became Albert Cashier and joined the 95th Illinois infantry.

Albert's army comrades remembered him as being small, tough, fearless and a deadly shot with a rifle. He liked to jump out of

trenches and taunt the other side (the Confederate Army). Once, when he was captured by the Confederates, Albert overpowered his captor and raced back to the Union lines.

After three years of war, Albert was demobilised (left the army), settled in the town of Saunemin, Illinois and acquired a house. He also enjoyed an army pension and the right to vote, and he worked for a living. Jennie Hodgers would not have been able to do any of those things. When Albert's health began to fail in 1913, he was moved to a retired Soldiers' and Sailors' Home. Two nurses revealed the truth about Albert's past gender and there was a national uproar. The government claimed that this elderly 'woman' was a fraud, could not have fought in the Civil War and cancelled his pension. However, Albert's former comrades in the 95th rallied around and confirmed that he had indeed been a Civil War soldier, and a very good one.

Albert's story, unfortunately, does not have a happy ending. His mental health had been in decline, and he spent the last two years of his life in a psychiatric hospital where he was forced to wear women's clothing. However, when he died, his former comrades insisted that he be given a full military funeral. Today the gravestone of Albert Cashier recognises his previous life, and that he was 'Born Jennie Hodgers in Clogherhead, Ireland'.

PHOTO

NAME ALBERT CASHIER
(BORN JENNIE HODGERS)
(1843-1915)

OCCUPATION SOLDIER

UNLIKELY TO SAY:	'Lovely colour, Confederate grey.'
LIKES:	The military life
DISLIKES:	Trying to live life as a woman
CLAIM TO FAME:	One of an estimated 400 women to change gender and fight in the US Civil War

PATRICK McLOUGHLIN AND PETER O'RILEY

If only they had realised the value of what they discovered!

I N 1859, FRIENDS Patrick McLoughlin and Peter O'Riley, two Irish immigrants to the USA, went in search of gold in the wilds of the western American state of Nevada. They didn't find any, but they did find plenty of silver. Unfortunately, they didn't know what they'd discovered and allowed themselves to be talked out of a huge fortune by someone who did.

Miners and prospectors (people who use pans to sieve for gold in riverbeds) are always looking for something called a 'lode'. That's a deposit of precious metal which could make you very rich indeed. The next step up, however, is the real pay-off. That happens when you hit upon something called 'the mother lode', which, as the name suggests, is the mother of all lodes and can lead to riches beyond the dreams of even the liveliest imaginations.

In 1848, gold was discovered in California, causing thousands of people from all over America to race to the state as fast as they could. This was called the California Gold Rush of 1849 (the San Francisco football team 'the 49ers' is called after it). Well, there was another gold rush a few years later in the neighbouring state of Nevada, to the east of California. Patrick and Peter, decided to try their luck there. But when they got to Nevada all the good 'claims' (working areas) were already taken.

They were left to scrabble around in a region called Six Mile Canyon that no one else could be bothered with because they figured there was no gold there.

When they started digging, they came across a strange black sandy gooey substance that they didn't recognise. They didn't get too excited about it and kept on looking for gold. But another miner working nearby knew exactly what it was they had found. His name was Henry Comstock and he recognised the thick black goo as a substance (an 'ore') from which pure silver could be extracted. He might not have been much of a miner, but Comstock was a smooth talker. He managed to convince the two Irishmen that he owned the land they were mining (he didn't). He 'generously' offered, because of all the hard work they'd been putting in, to give each

of them one-sixth of whatever the mine produced, while suggesting that it would probably be one-sixth of nothing. Even more generously, he offered to give them a few dollars for their share. McLoughlin decided to cash in very quickly and sold his share for what must have seemed like a fortune at the time, $3,500. O'Riley hung on for a little longer and managed to get $50,000 for his stake. What they didn't realise was that they had struck a mother lode that would, over a number of years, produce millions and millions of dollars worth of silver.

But at least this precious and famous deposit of silver ore would become known as the McLoughlin/O'Riley Lode after the two Irishmen who discovered it, right? Well, no, actually – to this day it is famous as the Comstock Lode.

PHOTO

NAME PATRICK MCLOUGHLIN AND PETER O'RILEY (MID-19TH CENTURY)

OCCUPATION MINERS

LIKELY TO SAY:	'Give us back our mine.'
LIKES:	Silver
DISLIKES:	Smooth-talking conmen
CLAIM TO FAME:	Two Irishmen conned out of their share of one of the biggest silver mines in history

WILLIAM MULHOLLAND

The man who enabled Los Angeles to grow,
by bringing water to the city.

IN 1913 THE Belfast-born William Mulholland had the greatest triumph of his life when the artificial river (aqueduct) he had designed and built brought drinking water from northern California to the growing city of Los Angeles (LA). However, in 1928 a dam he had designed and built near LA burst, sending millions of gallons of water and sludge into a nearby canyon and drowning more than 400 people.

William had moved from Belfast to Dublin as a child and left Ireland at the age of 15 to work as a sailor. In 1878, he arrived in the hot and sleepy southern Californian city of Los Angeles. It was growing, but because it was built in what amounted to little more than a desert, there was an upper limit to how much more it could grow. Without a greater supply of water, the city would be unable to support a population of more than about 250,000 people. When, after years of hard manual work and self-education as an engineer, William took over the city's Department of Water and Power, he decided to do something about the lack of water that was holding back the development of LA.

He looked north, to the valley of the Owens River in central California. He quietly bought up the water rights to the river that flowed there, and which was used to irrigate (meaning to supply with water) the orange groves of the Owens Valley. Before the people of the valley knew what was happening, William, on behalf of the city of LA, started building an aqueduct that would take the Owens Valley water away from their orange groves. The project took eight years to complete and was an amazing engineering achievement.

However, it angered the people of Owens Valley so much that they made numerous attempts to blow up the aqueduct. Once, after their bombs caused some damage, William expressed sorrow at the destruction of the orange groves of the Owens Valley, but only 'because now there are no longer enough trees to hang all the troublemakers who live there'.

In 1913, William's great project was completed. At the official opening of the aqueduct, the people of LA were invited to come and see the water pour into their reservoir. As it arrived, the Irish engineer told the assembled crowd, 'There it is, take it.' He was a hero in LA, but a villain in the Owens Valley.

Fifteen years later, however, William was a villain in LA as well, after the St Francis Dam, which he had also designed and built, began to spring leaks. He ignored warnings that there was a problem. Then, on 12 March 1928, the dam burst. At an inquiry investigating the resulting deaths, William said that he was so ashamed that he actually envied the people who had died, which probably did not go down well with their surviving relatives. His reputation was in tatters and he retired a broken man.

Certainly, no one in the Owens Valley had any sympathy for the Irish engineer. To them, it was pure karma (where the bad things you do eventually come back to haunt you).

PHOTO

NAME WILLIAM MULHOLLAND
(1855-1935)

OCCUPATION ENGINEER

DEFINITELY SAID:	'There it is, take it.'
LIKES:	Water
DISLIKES:	Dams
CLAIM TO FAME:	Brought water to Los Angeles from more than 200 miles away

I.W.
Votes
for
Women.
F.L.

MARGARET 'GRETTA' COUSINS

She played a role in the independence
of Ireland ... and of India.

MARGARET COUSINS, KNOWN to her family and friends as Gretta, is 100 per cent Irish but she is also claimed by India. In Ireland, Gretta was a suffragist (a campaigner for voting rights for women). In India, where she spent the last 40 years of her life, she was the first female magistrate (a type of judge), but she also made another lasting contribution to her adopted home. We'll come to that later.

As a young girl in Roscommon, one of 14 children, she could see that it was a man's world. She often said that she would have much preferred to have been born a boy. But it was very lucky for Irish and Indian women that she wasn't. She studied music in Dublin in her twenties and got involved as a leader of the campaign to give Irish women the franchise (the right to vote). She married James Cousins in 1903 and inspired him to become a feminist, while he inspired her to become a vegetarian. Theirs was a real partnership of equals.

Gretta was an excellent hammer thrower; however, her exploits did not take place on sports fields, but close to government buildings. During suffragist protests, campaigning for the franchise for women, she broke quite a few windows and ended up in jail more than once. She served time in Mountjoy and Tullamore prisons. Not a good look for a future judge/magistrate, you might think!

While in prison she went on hunger strike and certainly got the attention of the authorities. In 1918, women finally got the vote in British and Irish elections. It didn't do Margaret any good, however, as she and James had emigrated to India in 1915. Gretta became headmistress of a girls' school there and began to campaign against the 'child' marriages of very young Indian girls, as well as for the franchise for Indian women.

It was in 1923 that Margaret was invited to become a magistrate. She accepted the challenge of being (for a while, at least) the only female judge in the huge nation of India. In the 1930s, she defied the country's British colonial rulers by calling for independence for India. True to form, she ended up in jail again, this time for almost a year. While there, just so as not to be idle, she went on a hunger strike again and fought for improved conditions for women prisoners.

And she didn't neglect her musical talents either. In 1919, she was responsible for the melody that went on to become the national anthem of an independent India in 1947. A truly remarkable Irish woman.

PHOTO

NAME MARGARET 'GRETTA' COUSINS
(1878-1954)

OCCUPATION(S) SUFFRAGIST,
HUNGER STRIKER,
MAGISTRATE,
COMPOSER

UNLIKELY TO SAY:	'Pass the pork chops, James.'
LIKES:	Rights for women, music
DISLIKES:	People who tried to get in her way
CLAIM TO FAME:	Helped secure votes for Irish women and became the first female judge in an Indian court of law

MARY, LADY HEATH

The feminist flyer who broke through
the glass ceiling ... in her airplane.

THERE IS A certain type of person who is determined to be themselves and just doesn't give a toss what anyone else thinks of them. Mary, Lady Heath (born Sophie Mary Peirce-Evans in 1896) was one of those. She was a superb international athlete: a record-breaking high jumper and javelin thrower who could have competed in the Olympics except that, guess what, women were not allowed to compete in Olympic athletics events until 1928.

In between all the throwing and jumping, she got a degree in science and worked as a military messenger in the First World War. She also learned to fly a plane when she was in her twenties. She was bitten by the flying bug and wanted to show that women were just as capable as men of being professional pilots. While women in those days were allowed to fly (otherwise we would never have heard of the great Amelia Earhart), they were not permitted to carry passengers.

She was married three times (once to Sir James Heath, hence her name) and divorced twice. She was incredibly flamboyant (a bit of a show-off) and had no intention of trying to act like a man just to be allowed to fly for a living. She liked to show up for her flights wearing a jaw-dropping mink coat, a string of pearls and high heels, and then take off into the skies.

Her greatest adventure was an amazing flight in 1928 that began in Capetown in South Africa and ended in London. Ten thousand miles in a flimsy aircraft. The journey was supposed to take her three weeks – instead, it took three months. She flew in an open cockpit with little protection from the extremes of heat she encountered along the way. A few days into the flight, she crashed in Zimbabwe, then known as Rhodesia. The journey took so long that some newspapers reported she was dead. But she survived, made it to London and later forced the (male) authorities to grant her a commercial pilot's licence.

She was the first woman to be allowed to fly commercially, although she did not find it easy to get flying jobs. She died in an accident (on a bus, not in an aircraft) at the tragically early age of 42.

In the 1930s, she had returned to Ireland and trained a number of the pilots who went on to fly for our national airline, Aer Lingus, so she left a flying legacy in the country of her birth. In 1998, the Irish government issued a postage stamp in her honour.

PHOTO

NAME MARY, LADY HEATH,
AKA SOPHIE MARY PEIRCE-EVANS
(1896-1939)

OCCUPATION(S) ATHLETE,
PILOT

UNLIKELY TO SAY:	'I wonder is that the Nile … or the Thames?'
LIKES:	Flying
DISLIKES:	Men who tried to stop her from flying
CLAIM TO FAME:	First person to fly across the continent of Africa, from south to north, in an open cockpit aircraft

PART 7

UNDERRATED ROGUES

'Into Each Life Some Rain Must Fall' is the title of a song that, like the people you are about to meet in this section, you probably will not have heard of. This is because it was recorded in 1944, when your grandparents were chisellers. I only mention it because it seems appropriate, as we move to look at the members of the Rogues' Gallery (a museum of images of really bad people) who brought a lot of rain into a good many lives. The fact that sometimes this included their own lives does not excuse their appalling behaviour one little bit. Reading about them will confirm that not every Irish person of historical importance was a saint. Some of those in our country's distinguished and illustrious past were jewel thieves, pickpockets, embezzlers, witches, bodysnatchers, evicting landlords, highwaymen, rogue bishops and untrustworthy politicians. However, although they are probably best forgotten, their stories are all very interesting and offer us valuable lessons in how we should NOT behave.

Hold your nose and say hello to these bygone baddies of Irish history.

ALICE KYTELER

Misunderstood or maleficent?
She kept losing husbands and
was accused of witchcraft.

THE STORY OF Alice Kyteler of Kilkenny and her stepchildren is like a Grimm (or just grim) fairy tale, set 450 years before the Grimm brothers were even born.

You might think Alice's married life got off to a bad start when she married an outlaw sometime around 1280, but actually that was his name, William Outlaw. (I kid you not. It was just a name, however, not a job description.) He was a wealthy merchant and moneylender, and his brother, Roger Outlaw, would become the highest legal official in the country, the Lord Chancellor of Ireland. Alice's second husband, Adam Blund – whom she married around the year 1300, after William's death – was also a

wealthy merchant and moneylender. Then when Adam died, around 1309, she was married again, to Richard de Valle from Tipperary. Are you beginning to see a pattern emerging? (No, it is not as innocent as the coincidence of marrying a couple of moneylenders).

Well, the children of her fourth husband, John le Poer, certainly detected a pattern when their own father fell ill. They had not taken a shine to their stepmother. They accused Alice of murdering her previous husbands by poisoning and sorcery, and of attempting to poison their dad. They pointed out that Alice had managed to have their father change his will, leaving his money to Alice and her son by her first husband,

also called William Outlaw (sorry if all the outlaws are doing your head in, but that's the last of them).

Alice was put on trial for sacrificing animals, organising a coven of witches, making magic powders from the body parts of children, hanging out with demons and, oh yes, killing her first three husbands. Other members of her supposed coven were charged and tried along with her. One of them, Alice's servant Petronilla de Meath, was publicly flogged and then burned at the stake. Rather than wait around in Kilkenny, lovely and all as the city is, Alice decided that it was time to see the world. She fled and managed to disappear from history.

Now, it is possible that Alice was a witch. It is also possible that she poisoned her husbands. But there is another possibility: one of the many ways of getting the better of a woman in the Middle Ages was to accuse her of being a witch. How could they possibly prove they were not guilty of witchcraft? Many hundreds of unfortunate and completely non-demonic women all over Europe, and later in North America, failed to prove their innocence and were burned alive as witches.

Perhaps this was a fairy tale in which the stepchildren were Maleficent, and the stepmother was Sleeping Beauty.

PHOTO

NAME ALICE KYTELER
      (13TH/14TH CENTURY)

OCCUPATION(S) WIDOW,
              WITCH(?)

UNLIKELY TO SAY:	'Can I have the blood of a Christian and four newts' eyes to go?'
LIKES:	Rich husbands
DISLIKES:	Stepchildren
CLAIM TO FAME:	The first Irishwoman to be condemned for witchcraft

MILER MAGRATH

He took bribes, spied on
his neighbours and was probably
the worst bishop ever.

IF YOU'RE ROMAN CATHOLIC and you've had your Confirmation, then you'll have met your local bishop. I'm sure he (and it was definitely a 'he') was a nice man. Even if he wasn't, trust me on this, there's no chance that he's anything like Miler Magrath. Is your bishop married with nine children? Whoa!!! No, I thought not. That kind of thing is hard to hide these days. If he was, you would probably have heard.

Miler was born in County Fermanagh in 1522. In 1565 he became Roman Catholic bishop of the diocese of Down and Connor in his native Ulster. With the job came a pretty good income. So far, so ordinary. But then he managed to acquire quite a few more dioceses over the years and, of course,

the money that went with them. In 1571, he was promoted when he took over as Archbishop of Cashel. Archbishops are more important than mere bishops. By the time of his death, it was almost easier to count the number of Irish dioceses of which Miler had NOT been bishop.

Another thing: no one, including Miler himself, was entirely sure if he was a Catholic or a Protestant bishop – for almost ten years he seems to have been a bit of both. So, it was distinctly uncool, at least from the pope's point of view, when it was discovered that he had married a woman named Áine O'Meara and had nine children. The Catholic Church has a pretty strict rule about priests: they are supposed to practise

something called celibacy, meaning no marrying or having romantic relationships. It's a bit like a goalkeeper handling the ball outside the penalty area – not allowed. If you want to marry you can still be a good Catholic, you just can't be a priest at the same time. Miler definitely lacked a bit of practice on that one.

While Miler managed to survive everything that was thrown at him (he changed sides in wars, disputes and fights whenever it suited him) he was disliked equally by Irish Catholics and Irish Protestants. To the Catholics he was a traitor to their religion; to the Protestants he was a thief and a downright bad egg who drank far too much.

He wasn't wildly popular with his parishioners either. After 35 years as Archbishop of Cashel, his flock was down to one! If he had been an actual shepherd, he would have starved to death.

While there is a monument to his memory on the grounds of the cathedral in Cashel, it doesn't really count when it comes to commemorating him. That's because he had it built himself. And, just in case you needed some solid proof that 'Only the good die young', Miler lived to be almost one hundred years old! Just imagine how much damage he managed to do in that space of time.

PHOTO

NAME MILER MAGRATH
(1522-1622)

OCCUPATION REALLY DODGY BISHOP

DIOCESES:	Down and Connor, Clogher, Waterford and Lismore, Cashel, Achonry, Killala … there are probably more but I'm just going to stop right here.
LIKES:	Collecting dioceses and the money from those dioceses, backing both sides in a war
DISLIKES:	Priestly celibacy
CLAIM TO FAME:	Probably holds the record for accumulating dioceses

CAPTAIN THOMAS BLOOD

The Meathman who almost got away
with the British Crown Jewels.

IN 17TH-CENTURY ENGLAND, you could be hanged for cutting down a tree unless it was yours. And if your crime involved an offence against the king (Spoiler alert! If you are eating, please stop NOW!) you would be half-hanged, cut down, and then your entrails (otherwise known as your guts/ intestines) would be removed while you looked on with interest. Then your head would be chopped off and your remains cut into four pieces, though you'd probably have lost interest at that stage. This was called being 'hanged, drawn and quartered'. Oh yes, sorry, I left something out: your various bits and pieces would then be stuck on the end of a pike (a sort of spear), or on top of a pointy railing, and displayed in public to discourage anyone else from committing an offence against the king. You have to admit, it was pretty discouraging. (OK, you can start eating again now, I'm done.)

I mention this by way of pointing out how lucky Thomas Blood – born in Sarney, County Meath in 1618 – was when he was caught making off with the British Crown Jewels from the Tower of London in 1671.

The plan was that Thomas would befriend the keeper of the jewels, a man named Talbot Edwards. Thomas managed to get sufficiently chummy with Talbot, and he gained access to the jewels, along with two friends (the Gardaí call those kinds of people accomplices).

They then jumped the poor keeper with the aid of a mallet and started to scoop up the king's ceremonial crown, sceptre and orb (a sort of golden globe). As they made their getaway, Talbot came to and managed to shout a warning. The thieves were caught red-handed (gold-handed, really) and Thomas was hauled before the king himself.

You'd think that the king, in a rage, would have immediately sentenced Blood to be hanged, drawn and quartered, given the seriousness of his crime. But no ... as a matter of fact, King Charles II was so impressed by the smooth-talking Meathman (we're all like that in Meath) that he gave him a valuable estate in Ireland.

'What?' I hear you say! 'He did what?'

'He gave him a valuable estate in Ireland,' I reply.

'Why did he do that?' I hear you ask.

Maybe Charles was having a good day and didn't want to spoil the vibe. But there was a rumour at the time that the king was in need of money and that Thomas Blood was actually stealing the jewels on his behalf. You see, the Crown Jewels don't belong to individual kings or queens, but to the British monarchy; they have to be available for the coronation of future British monarchs. So Charles II couldn't just sell them off to make a few bob. But, if someone stole them ... You see where I'm going with this?

Maybe Thomas Blood was a simple thief, but maybe he was working for the king. What do you think?

PHOTO

NAME CAPTAIN THOMAS BLOOD
      (1618-1680)

OCCUPATION FAILED JEWEL THIEF

LIKES:	Expensive trinkets
DISLIKES:	Talbot Edwards
CLAIM TO FAME:	Tried, and failed, to make off with the Crown Jewels from the Tower of London

JAMES MacLAINE

The 'gentleman highwayman' who was
unfailingly polite as he robbed you blind.

THERE WAS AN important tradition among the upper classes of Britain and Ireland in the 18th and 19th centuries that the first-born son would inherit the family estate and all other male offspring would, more or less, fend for themselves. As for the female offspring, well they had better find a husband, or else … The second/third/fourth sons would either have commissions in the military bought for them (they would then become army or naval officers) or, if they were even slightly nerdy, they might end up as clergymen in the Church of England or the Church of Ireland.

James MacLaine was the second son of a highly respectable Presbyterian family in Monaghan in the 1720s, but he plotted a rather unusual route for a second son. He had a nasty habit of taking money from family members and friends that had been given to help set him up in a real profession. Instead, he would spend it on living the high life. So, it didn't take long for him to run out of relatives and friends who were prepared to invest any money in his future. Rather than going into the church or the army, he decided to take up the profession of robbing people and became a highwayman. Back in the 18th century, that line of work was surprisingly popular, even though many highwaypersons (there were one or two women) never got the opportunity to retire as they were hanged long before they reached retirement age.

James joined the Premier League of highwaymen (I made that one up) when he teamed up with fellow Irishman William Plunkett and started to rob travellers on

the outskirts of London. Back in those days, London was so small that places like Hyde Park and Hampstead Heath, which are now fairly central, were on the outskirts of the city.

To disguise themselves, the two men would wear elaborate Venetian masks (the kind that you would normally see at a masked ball or an opera). James became famous for being well-spoken and extremely polite when he was robbing people, which earned him the nickname 'The Gentleman Highwayman'. Fortunately, everyone handed over their money to him without having to be asked twice, so his status as a 'gentleman' was never put to the test, because he was never obliged to hurt anyone!

All good things must come to an end, though, as do all bad things. In August 1750, James was caught and put on trial for his life. Such was his reputation for courtesy that many of his victims would not give evidence against him. But he was convicted anyway. He went to the scaffold (that's where they hang people) at Tyburn – a popular venue for executions, also on the outskirts of London – on 3 October 1750 and a huge crowd turned out to see him breathe his last.

His accomplice, William Plunkett, was more fortunate. He managed to escape and may have got all the way to America, where he is reported to have died more than 40 years after the hanging of James MacLaine. Some people have all the luck.

PHOTO

NAME JAMES MACLAINE
(1724–1750)

....

OCCUPATION HIGHWAYMAN

LIKELY TO SAY:	'Your money or your life … if you wouldn't mind awfully.'
LIKES:	The high life
DISLIKES:	The scaffold
CLAIM TO FAME:	Successful (until caught) 18th-century London highwayman

GEORGE BARRINGTON

Robbing from the rich to feed ...
George Barrington.

UNLIKE ROBIN HOOD, when George Barrington stole, he did not give his proceeds to the poor: he kept them for himself. He had a lifestyle to maintain, after all. He was a gentleman thief, and being a gentleman in the 18th century cost money. Except, in George's case, it was other people's money which kept him in the style to which he was accustomed.

George was originally from Maynooth, County Kildare. He was well brought up and got an expensive education. How did he repay his doting parents? By stabbing another student, stealing from one of his teachers and running away to join the circus. All before he was 16.

He soon found out that there wasn't much of a living to be made as a circus performer.

After thinking over his options, he decided that robbing people offered the greatest reward for the least amount of effort. He began his life of crime in Limerick, but soon spread his wings and was thieving in other parts of the country. He fled to London when things got too hot for him in Ireland.

Because he was well-educated and well-spoken, he was able to pose as a gentleman and enter upper-crust London society, where the richest pickings were to be had. One of his specialities was robbing the wealthy in theatres or opera houses. In 1775, he relieved a Russian count of a golden snuff box that was inset with diamonds – the box would be worth the equivalent of more than €1 million today. George might well have thought he was doing his victim a favour, helping the count to give up his snuff habit,

but it is more likely that he thought he would be able to retire early when he sold it.* However, he was arrested when the theft was discovered. Luckily for him, the Russian nobleman didn't press charges, so George lived to rob another day.

On a couple of occasions when he was nabbed, George used his charm to talk his way out of trouble. His luck finally ran out in 1791. Or did it? Yes, he was finally arrested and found guilty; yes, he was sentenced to be transported on a convict ship to Australia (it wasn't as nice a place then as it is now – it was reserved for convicted prisoners), but on his way there, he heard that some of the prisoners planned to seize the ship, and he ratted out the mutineers to the ship's captain. In return, he was given a pretty soft time during his period as a prisoner in Australia, as he was put in charge of his fellow convicts. When he died in 1804, George was ... wait for it ... a senior policeman.

That might seem like an odd twist. But it makes complete sense when you think about it. I mean, who knows more about how to stop crime than a former criminal?

*Snuff, by the way, is finely ground tobacco that people stuffed up their nostrils in the 18th and 19th centuries. Nope, sorry, I can't help you there. I don't get it either.

PHOTO

NAME GEORGE BARRINGTON
(1755-1804)

OCCUPATION GENTLEMAN THIEF

LIKELY TO SAY:	'You've got to pick a pocket or two …'
LIKES:	Wallets
DISLIKES:	Policemen
CLAIM TO FAME:	A talented pickpocket who preyed on the rich

JOSEPH KAVANAGH

The Irish cobbler who stormed
the Bastille and started the
French Revolution.

TRUST AN IRISHMAN to muscle in on one of the greatest moments in French history.

France celebrates its independence on 14 July every year. They call it Bastille Day because it commemorates the attack on a famous prison in Paris, the French capital, that held jailed opponents of French kings. By 1789, the French poor (and there were plenty of them) had become sick and tired of being taxed, starved and abused by kings who built fabulous palaces for themselves and lived in luxury, and rich noblemen who abused and mistreated them. They were angry and they weren't going to take any more. When it comes to angry mobs, it is not unusual to have an Irishman in the middle of it all. This was the case when the spark was lit in Paris and the city exploded. Joseph Kavanagh was there to (briefly) lead the revolution.

The poor of Paris rose up in rebellion against King Louis XVI. When Louis sent his army against them, the rebels were desperate for weapons. They heard that there was a store of arms and ammunition in the Bastille prison and decided to attack the jail and take the weapons. They were led by a bootmaker named Joseph Kavanagh, which is not a very French name. That is because he was from Carlow ... or Clare ... or Wexford. No one seems to know which, and all three counties are happy to claim him – at least for his exploits on 14 July 1789 (not so much after that!). Joseph and his followers managed to

capture the Bastille and release the last six political prisoners being held there.

After the storming of the Bastille, there was no going back. The French Revolution had truly begun, and would lead to the widespread use of the guillotine and the beheading of many French aristocrats, including King Louis XVI himself.

Why then, you might ask, is Joseph Kavanagh lumped in with the 'baddies'? In the Republic of Ireland, deposing kings would generally be seen as a good cause, although chopping off their heads would be frowned upon. Joe is included in our list of baddies because the French Revolution quickly turned on itself and threw up leaders who were as ruthless and brutal as any evil king or nobleman.

The most notorious of these was a leader named Maximilien Robespierre, who took charge of the country during what became known as the 'Terror' – this was when thousands of supporters of the initial 1789 revolution were themselves beheaded as Robespierre took control. Joe Kavanagh, as a revolutionary policeman, was a servant of Robespierre and took part in a horrible massacre of prisoners in Paris in 1792. After Robespierre himself was guillotined in 1794, Joe, very sensibly, disappeared from view.

He may even have headed back to Carlow … or Clare … or Wexford. If you come across any local tales of a cobbler with a French accent arriving unexpectedly in your town in the 1790s, that might be him!

PHOTO

NAME JOSEPH KAVANAGH
(LATE 18TH CENTURY)

OCCUPATION(S) COBBLER,
FRENCH REVOLUTIONARY

LIKELY TO SAY:	'Vive la révolution! Off with his head.'
LIKES:	The people, the guillotine
DISLIKES:	Kings and aristocrats
CLAIM TO FAME:	Led the attack on the Bastille prison on 14 July 1789 that kicked off the French Revolution

WILLIAM BURKE AND WILLIAM HARE

The notorious Edinburgh bodysnatching firm of 'Burke and Hare'.

BACK IN 18TH- and early 19th-century Britain and Ireland, if you were hanged for a crime there was no guarantee that you would ever be buried. Instead, your body could be sent to a medical school for trainee surgeons to practise on your remains as they studied anatomy (the science of the human body). But, although there were far more hangings back then than in, for example, the second half of the 19th century, there were still never enough victims of the rope to satisfy the needs of these medical schools. So, a new 'profession' was created, that of the bodysnatcher or 'the resurrection man'. They would hang around graveyards and watch out for new burials. They would then return late at

night, dig up the body and sell it to the anatomists for a tidy sum of money. To avoid the resurrection men, family members would often stand guard over the graves of loved ones until the body had decomposed enough to make it useless to the graverobbers. (Apologies, yet again, if you're eating.)

Grisly stuff. But not nearly as dreadful as the activities of two Irish bodysnatchers in Scotland in the 1820s. They were William Burke, from Tyrone, and William Hare, from Armagh. Burke was Hare's lodger in the Scottish capital city of Edinburgh, but he had a peculiar way of paying the rent. He and his landlord began doing night work as bodysnatchers. The tools of their trade were

a couple of sturdy shovels and a hand cart for transporting corpses.

But there were just never enough fresh corpses. So Burke and Hare took the next logical step to save their livelihoods: they set aside their shovels and took up cudgels instead. A cudgel is like a small baseball bat and can be quite uncomfortable if applied to the base of the skull with considerable force. In fact, it can be quite fatal, and that was the intention of Burke and Hare. To make up for the lack of funerals, they began to murder people (usually the poor and/ or lonely), toss them on their handcart and take them, still warm, to the surgeon and teacher of anatomy, Dr Robert Knox of the Edinburgh University Medical School, where they were paid seven pounds ten shillings per body (that's more than €500 today).

Knox was very good at not asking questions about this seemingly endless supply.

Fortunately, the Scottish police were much more curious than the professor of anatomy. They eventually caught up with Burke and Hare, but not before the two ex-bodysnatchers had murdered at least 16 people. The two men got careless with their last victim and left her body lying around for witnesses to see. Hare literally got away with murder when he agreed to give evidence against Burke, who was hanged in January 1829.

Guess what happened to Burke's body? Correct – it was brought to a medical school and dissected by an anatomy student. Now that's something called irony. Or maybe karma?

PHOTO

NAME WILLIAM BURKE (1792-1829),

WILLIAM HARE (BORN BETWEEN 1792 AND 1804, DATE OF DEATH UNKNOWN)

OCCUPATION(S) GRAVE ROBBERS, MURDERERS

UNLIKELY TO SAY:	'Rest in peace.'
LIKES:	Corpses
DISLIKES:	The hangman's noose
CLAIM TO FAME:	Serial killers who 'provided' corpses for medical research

JOHN SADLIER

Couldn't be trusted as a politician,
couldn't be trusted as a banker.

'**E**MBEZZLE', **WHAT A** wonderful word. It sounds like it should have some connection with keeping bees, but it's actually to do with keeping money that doesn't belong to you. This is a lot easier – but definitely not encouraged – if you own a bank, as John Sadlier did. John was the proprietor of the Tipperary Joint Stock Bank at a time when apparently anyone could open an office, claim it was a bank and invite all and sundry to lodge their money. You would be surprised at how many people handed over their life savings to someone who smiled at them, looked them in the eye and said, 'Trust me, I'm a banker.'

John Sadlier was from Tipperary, and the customers he bilked (cheated of their hard-earned cash) should probably have been forewarned by his short career in politics.

He was first elected to the House of Commons in London as an Irish member of the British parliament (an MP) in 1847, and then again in 1852. Second time around, he made a solemn pledge to his fellow Irish members of parliament, who were part of something called the Independent Irish Party, that he would not accept a job in government and would, from his place in the opposition benches, faithfully represent the people who had voted for him. That is where MPs who are not members of the government sit, and usually hurl abuse at ministers with responsibility for spending taxpayers' money.

How did that promise go? Not too well really. Within days of the new parliament assembling, John Sadlier had been offered a job as one of those money-spending government ministers, and had grabbed hold

of it like a rugby player latches on to any pair of legs running in his general direction. He was condemned as a traitor by Irish voters, and his effigy was burned at public meetings.

Four years later, the people of Tipperary would have been more inclined to burn the man himself rather than simply set fire to his effigy. That was because John Sadlier liked the good life. The good life costs lots of money. Rather than earn it, he stole it from his customers. In other words, he had long been embezzling money from his own bank. He then cheated his customers twice over by taking himself off to Hampstead Heath in London and drinking a deadly draught of the lethal poison prussic acid instead of facing their wrath.

He would probably be mostly forgotten today had Charles Dickens not decided to base one of his characters on Sadlier. Mr Merdle from Dickens's *Little Dorrit*, is a banker who is feared and respected in London until it is discovered that he has been ripping off his customers.

Sadlier was buried in an unmarked grave in the famous Highgate Cemetery in London. This unusual step was taken because it was feared that a number of investors in his Tipperary Joint Stock Bank were anxious to discover the whereabouts of his grave. Just so that they could pay their respects, of course ...

PHOTO

NAME JOHN SADLIER
(1813–1856)

OCCUPATION(S) BANKER,
POLITICIAN,
EMBEZZLER ON A GRAND SCALE

LIKELY TO SAY:	'Why don't you let me look after your savings?'
LIKES:	Other people's money, breaking his word
DISLIKES:	Charles Dickens
CLAIM TO FAME:	Used his Tipperary Joint Stock Bank to steal money from his customers

THE MARQUESS
OF CLANRICARDE

He was such a cruel landlord that
even other landlords hated him.

HAVE YOU EVER wondered where the word 'peer' comes from? No? Don't care? OK so, let's start again, shall we?

The word peer has a couple of different meanings. A peer of the realm, for example, is someone with a title like lord, earl or duke. But a peer, oddly enough, also applies to someone who is your equal in status, like your classmates. So, for example, if you should ever be unfortunate enough to stand trial before a jury, you will be judged by 12 of your peers – people who are equal to you in status.

Hubert George de Burgh-Canning was a peer (in the first sense) who was judged by his peers (in the second sense), and they really loathed him. Fortunately for him, he was never judged in a court of law, just by his fellow aristocrats. And by his tenants. They hated him too. In fact, it's probably fair to say that pretty much everyone he ever came in contact with disliked Hubert George de Burgh-Canning, 2nd Marquess of Clanricarde.

Clanricarde (let's just call him that – everyone who loathed him did) came from an ancient Irish family who had been granted land in Ireland almost as far back as the Norman invasion. Not that he spent much time in Ireland. He was what is known as an absentee landlord, which meant that he spent most of his life out of the country and

had an agent who looked after his estates and collected rents for him. Clanricarde owned a very big estate, more than 57,000 acres (around 230 square kilometres), in County Galway. Not that he ever saw it. He just took the rent money and hoarded it in London. He didn't even bother to visit Galway for his own mother's funeral.

His tenants despised him because he charged high rents and liked to evict people who were unable to pay. Not that he got involved in the evictions himself; he had his agent do that for him. When his agent's life was threatened, Clanricarde said that he wasn't scared by that sort of talk. Easy for him to say, of course, he wasn't going to be shot. For the record, his agent, a man named Blake, was actually murdered. Clanricarde, who probably didn't even send flowers to the funeral (he was really mean and miserly), just got another agent.

When the government tried to persuade Clanricarde to sell his Galway land, he refused. When they tried to force him to sell his land, almost the entire House of Commons voted in favour. However, they were unable to shift him until 1915, a year before his death.

Remember that word irony we've been throwing around a bit? Well, towards the end of his life, Clanricarde had a row with the landlord who owned the posh house he rented in London. He was evicted!

PHOTO

NAME HUBERT GEORGE DE BURGH-CANNING, 2ND MARQUESS OF CLANRICARDE (1832–1916)

OCCUPATION ABSENTEE IRISH LANDLORD

UNLIKELY TO SAY:	'Sure, you can just pay the rent when you've got the money.'
LIKES:	Money, money, money
DISLIKES:	His own landlord
CLAIM TO FAME:	Probably the nastiest landlord in the nasty history of nasty Irish landlords

MARY MALLON

'Typhoid' Mary, the carrier from Cookstown and the cook from hell.

WHEN SOMEONE HAS an infectious illness, like a cold, you tend to know all about it and you can steer well clear of them.* They cough until you think their lungs are going to pop out. They sneeze so loudly that the cat jumps three feet in the air, lands on your shoulders and claws you half to death. But there was a problem with Mary Mallon from Tyrone. It wasn't that she sneezed and coughed a lot – it was that she didn't.

Mary was what they call a 'carrier'. This meant that she carried the deadly disease of typhoid fever, but no one knew this because she showed no symptoms of her own. No high fever. No sweating buckets. As a result, she breezed through life passing the disease on to lots of other people, up to 50 of whom got sick and died. She couldn't be blamed for

infecting her first 'victims' because no one, not even Mary herself, knew that she was a deadly carrier. But that was not the case with her later victims: by then she knew exactly what risks they were running by coming in contact with her. However, they didn't.

In the early 1900s, Mary worked as a cook for several well-off families in New York State. When many of her employers came down with typhoid fever, it took a while for the medical profession to join the dots and figure out the connection. Rich people who lived in clean and hygienic houses didn't get typhoid, only the poor did. The rich, however, employed servants, and it turned out that these rich people in particular were all eating lethal meals cooked by Mary, who wasn't the best at washing her hands before she went to work. She managed to infect her employers

with the deadly salmonella bacteria that causes typhoid fever.

For the safety of others (Mary was absolutely fine herself) in 1907 she was isolated in a New York cottage for three years. This is called quarantine, and we all became very familiar with it during the Covid-19 pandemic. Mary was finally released on the condition that she would only work in a laundry and never so much as toast a slice of bread again for anyone other than herself. By 1915, however, the New York health authorities noticed a mysterious upward trend in the incidence of typhoid. They tracked down the cause: an Irish cook named Mary Brown. 'Typhoid Mary' was back

in business under a false name. This time she was left in quarantine until she died in 1938. Even then, the authorities weren't taking any chances. They didn't want to risk burial, so her body was cremated.

One last thing: the town in County Tyrone that Mary was from is called Cookstown! Seriously. There's that irony thing again.

*Did you know that we produce up to two litres of snot every day of our lives (which seems a bit on the low side for babies), and if you have a cold, you can produce twice as much? What a disgusting fact. You're welcome. Enjoy your dinner.

PHOTO

NAME MARY MALLON,
AKA MARY BROWN
(1869-1938)

OCCUPATION COOK,
CARRIER
(AND NOT OF VEGETABLES)

UNLIKELY TO SAY:	'Will sir have a deadly disease with that?'
LIKES:	Domestic employment
DISLIKES:	Handwashing
CLAIM TO FAME:	Spreading deadly typhoid without experiencing any symptoms herself

FRANK SHACKLETON

The chief suspect in the 1907 theft of the Irish Crown Jewels.

BORN IN KILDARE in 1874, Ernest Shackleton was a famous explorer whose extraordinary navigational skills saved the lives of all of the members of his ill-fated polar exploration in 1917. He led three expeditions to the Antarctic. Although too old to be conscripted into the British Army, he volunteered to fight in the First World War. He was honoured for his heroism and his achievements by nine different countries.

But we're not going to discuss Ernest here. No, we're going to talk about his younger brother, Frank, a much different kettle of fish. If you've got a younger brother, you are bound to sympathise with poor Ernest. Younger brothers are really annoying. I know this because I am one, though I doubt anyone could be as much of a nuisance to an older brother or sister as Frank Shackleton was to Ernest.

Frank was the black sheep of the Shackleton family. He got a decent enough start in life before he went to the bad. He joined the British Army and fought in the Boer War in South Africa in 1899. He had a good side-line as a genealogist (investigating people's family trees) and mixed a lot in high society in Dublin and London. But he also had access to the building in Dublin Castle (the Office of Arms) where a valuable stash of gold collars and jewelled stars and badges was stored. These so-called 'Irish Crown Jewels' (worth about €5 million today) belonged to a society of wealthy Irish aristocrats, the Knights of St Patrick. The jewels disappeared in the summer of 1907 and Shackleton, who owed a lot of people

a lot of money at the time, was suspected of being the inside man on the job. It was assumed, but never proven, that because he worked in the Office of Arms, he had provided the thieves with keys and then cleared off to London so that he was out of the country when the theft was committed. This gave him a good alibi.

Even though Frank never faced trial for stealing the jewels (no one did, and we don't know what happened to them), he still came to a sticky end. With his investments going south (a nice way of saying he had run out of money, was bankrupt and still owed a small fortune) he stole money from an elderly lady to whom he was supposed to be giving financial advice. With the police on his heels, he fled to Africa but was arrested and sent back to England. He spent more than a year in jail. After his release, his family (including big brother Ernest) set him up as an antique dealer named Frank Mellor, in the town of Chichester in Sussex.

Even though Frank's family knew not to trust him when it came to money. His sister reportedly would warn her children that on no account were they to lend Uncle Frank any money when he came to visit! Some leopards never change their spots.

Which neatly brings us on to the final section!

PHOTO

NAME FRANCIS RICHARD SHACKLETON, AKA FRANK MELLOR (1876-1941)

OCCUPATION(S) GENEALOGIST, FINANCIAL ADVISER, CONVICT, ANTIQUE DEALER, JEWEL THIEF(?)

MIGHT HAVE SAID:	'I'm having those.'
LIKES:	The good life
DISLIKES:	Prison uniforms
CLAIM TO FAME:	The chief suspect in the theft of the Irish Crown Jewels in 1907

PART 8

FORGOTTEN FUR AND FEATHERS

If you throw a stick in Ireland, a dog will bring it
back and beg you with its big brown eyes to throw it again.
If you try that with a cat, they will fix you with a
withering stare. But still, we love them both to distraction.

We have more cattle and sheep than people in Ireland.
Our horses seem to have the same status as sacred cows in
India. So, it stands to reason that there have been a number of
very interesting Irish animals over the years. Far too illustrious
to feature here are racehorses like the Epsom Derby winners
Shergar or Nijinsky. Or Arkle, who won three Cheltenham Gold
Cups in a row over fences and whose skeleton can be seen
on display in the Irish National Stud (where horses
go to make baby horses).

Get ready to meet a Hollywood star, a war hero, a rebel
and a noble dog, a roguish elephant and a horse with
his very own imposter.

GELERT

The Irish wolfhound still revered in Wales.

IRISH WOLFHOUNDS ARE the stuff of legend. We don't even know for certain if the ancient Irish wolfhound looked like the modern version of the animal. The current breed comes from two large dogs of the 1860s named Faust and Old Donagh owned by a man named George Graham. Together they produced the pups who went on to give us the huge furry wolfhounds we know and love today.

You've probably heard of the great Irish warrior hero Cú Chulainn who heroically defended Ulster against the forces of Queen Medb of Connacht during the Cattle Raid of Cooley. What people tend to forget, however, is that that wasn't always his name. He was born Setanta and acquired the name Cú Chulainn (the hound of Culann) when he killed the fierce guard dog of the blacksmith Culann with a sliotar (hurling ball) and offered to take over from the dog as the smith's protector. The unfortunate animal he replaced (who was only doing his job when he attacked Setanta) was probably an Irish wolfhound. As all the stories about Cú Chulainn are legends anyway, there is nowhere we can go to find out. So let's just assume he was a wolfhound.

The story of the Irish hound Gelert may also be a legend. Most historians think that it's just a folk tale. Nonetheless, it has become a huge part of the national culture of our neighbours in Wales. The story/legend goes that Gelert was a huge Irish guard dog, more than likely to have been a wolfhound, gifted in 1210 by King John of England to Llywelyn the Great, ruler of the province of Gwynedd in north Wales.

Llywelyn was a powerful Welsh warrior who became known as a 'Prince of the Welsh' and ruled his kingdom for almost 50 years. His son, Dafydd ap Llywelyn, was the first man to claim the title Prince of Wales.

While Gelert was a much-loved and faithful guard dog of Llywelyn's, their relationship came to a tragic end. One day, on returning from a hunt, Llywelyn discovered his child's cradle overturned. The baby was nowhere to be seen and Gelert's mouth was smeared with blood. Jumping to the conclusion that the hound had killed his child, Llywelyn took out his sword and killed the unfortunate animal in an angry gesture of revenge. As he did so, he heard the cries of his child and discovered the baby behind the upturned cradle. Lying beside the child was a dead wolf. Llywelyn realised, to his horror, that Gelert had killed the wolf while defending the infant. Grief-stricken, he buried his beloved Irish wolfhound in a touching ceremony. Legend has it that Llywelyn never smiled again, so remorseful was he for having killed his faithful Irish guard dog.

Gelert's legend lives on to this day in Wales and he even has a small, picturesque town named after him, Bedd Gelert (Gelert's grave), which is set in a beautiful Welsh river valley surrounded by the mountains of Snowdonia. The 'grave of Gelert' can be visited there – it bears two slate plaques, one in English, one in Welsh, telling the story of the courageous Irish wolfhound.

PHOTO

NAME GELERT
(EARLY 13TH CENTURY)

OCCUPATION GUARDING THE PROPERTY
OF LLYWELYN THE GREAT,
PRINCE OF GWYNEDD IN WALES

LIKELY TO SAY:	'Woof!'
UNLIKELY TO SAY:	Anything other than 'Woof!'
CLAIM TO FAME:	Saved the life of Llewelyn's child but lost his own life in the process

PRINCE TOM

The Dublin Zoo and
Trinity College elephant.

YOU MAY BE familiar with the expression 'the elephant in the room'. This means that there is an important matter which is bothering everyone, but no one wants to talk about it. However, in the case of Trinity College Dublin there actually is an elephant in the room. His name is Prince Tom and his skeleton is on display in the college Zoological Museum. That is one elephant in the room that everybody talks about.

Tom was an Indian elephant who came here in 1871 at a time when Britain took a lot of things from that part of the world and didn't give them back. He was a gift to Alfred, Duke of Edinburgh (Queen Victoria's second son), who, when he left India, took Tom with him on board the HMS *Galatea* on a journey to New Zealand. While in transit,

Tom earned his keep doing heavy lifting and was rewarded at the end of every day with a traditional tot of Royal Navy rum. Well, given his size, maybe a bit more than the usual ration. And no, it is definitely NOT a good idea to feed an elephant (or any animal) alcoholic beverages for their supper.

His later journey to Ireland was a bit of a disaster. He was put in the charge of an artillery corporal, William Paton. When Tom arrived in England and boarded a train everything went pear-shaped. As soon as the train got up to full speed, Tom panicked. He began kicking out the panels of his compartment and, in the process, crushed poor Corporal Paton to death.

As a resident of Dublin Zoo, Tom became a popular attraction. He gave lifts to children

on his back and was trained to 'buy' buns from the cake shop with coins provided by visitors. He collected these in his trunk and spent them on the treats.

Neither security nor health and safety seem to have been that important in the Dublin Zoological Gardens in the 1870s, as Prince Tom managed to escape from his compound on a couple of occasions. Fortunately, he was escorted back to the elephant house before doing any damage. Once, when his owner, the Duke of Edinburgh, visited Dublin, he asked the zoo to drop Tom off at the Viceregal Lodge in Phoenix Park (now Áras an Uachtaráin) so that he could have a look at his outsized pet. Tom's keepers gently suggested that perhaps the duke should drop in on Tom instead. Escorting a fully grown elephant through Phoenix Park might make people nervous, they explained.

Tom's years as a serious drinker with a sweet tooth didn't do much for his health and he died in 1882 at the age of 15. After his death he was transported on a huge float to Trinity College Zoological Museum where he has been the 'elephant in the room' ever since.

PHOTO

NAME PRINCE TOM
(1867–1882)

OCCUPATION(S) BEING AN ELEPHANT, OFFERING RIDES TO CHILDREN

MOST LIKELY TO SAY:	'Harrumph.'
LIKES:	Rum, sticky buns
DISLIKES:	Trains
CLAIM TO FAME:	Resident of Trinity College Dublin (permanent)

POPPET

The rebel dog of the
1916 Easter Rising.

ONE OF THE flags that flew in O'Connell Street during the Easter Rising of 1916 was the tricolour, as you would expect. The other was dark green and had the words 'Irish Republic' painted on it in gold lettering. It was homemade from an emerald-green bedspread and was created by stretching the bedspread very tightly across a grand piano so that the words could then be painted on its surface. All this was done in the house of the best-known female leader of the Rising, Countess Markievicz, a very aristocratic lady, but also an enthusiastic senior officer in the Irish Citizen Army. This was a small unit of Dublin workers and trade union members who fought alongside the Irish Volunteers and against the British Army in 1916. They wore dark green uniforms while the Irish Volunteers wore a lighter shade of green.

The flag is more than a hundred years old now, so you would hardly expect it to be in perfect condition today. But neither was it in very good nick as it was raised over the General Post Office on Easter Monday 1916, when the rebels took over the building and made it their headquarters. That was because a couple of chunks had been surgically removed by the teeth of a bored cocker spaniel called Poppet.

What had the flag done to in-cur the wrath of Poppet? (Dog pun #1.) Why did she hound the poor bedspread? (Dog pun #2.) Perhaps she was a supremely talented dog who wanted to play the piano and had to get rid of the bedspread first? OK, that's probably a bit far-fetched. Poppet belonged to Countess Markievicz and, by all accounts, could pretty much do as she liked.

The countess spoiled her rotten. The makers of the flag should consider themselves lucky that when it was raised over the GPO it didn't read 'Irish Repub—' courtesy of Poppet's canines (front teeth ... and dog pun #3). That's enough bad dog puns for now.

Poppet was very faithful to her mistress. She even went to jail with the countess when she was arrested in 1918. But the animal had been specially trained to growl at a British Army uniform (and stand to attention at the sight of a Volunteer or Irish Citizen Army uniform), so her jailers handed the cranky mutt over to the countess's sister, Eva, and were delighted to see the back of her.

The spaniel was not Ms Pop(pet)ularity. (That's not a dog pun.) She liked to bite, and not always playfully either. One of Ireland's great writers, Seán Ó Faoláin, who knew Countess Markievicz well, wrote that the spaniel was disliked intensely, 'as an old dog you'd love to root, and behind her [the countess's] back, Poppet did get an occasional root!' A 'root' is an old-fashioned term for ... well, you've probably guessed that it has something to do with the application of shoe-leather to the posterior regions.

When a statue was erected to Countess Markievicz in Townsend Street in Dublin, Poppet was included at her feet. The sculptor wisely chose not to depict the grumpy spaniel with two chunks of emerald-green bedspread sticking out of the side of her mouth.

PHOTO

NAME POPPET MARKIEVICZ
(C. 1916)

OCCUPATION REVOLUTIONARY HOUND
(CÚ RÉABHLÓIDEACH)

ANSWERS TO:	'Here, Poppy!'
LIKES:	Ankles, Countess Markievicz
DISLIKES:	British Army uniforms
CLAIM TO FAME:	The only dog of the 1916 Rising commemorated in a statue

CAIRBRE

The first Dublin-born
Hollywood movie star.

EVEN THOUGH HE was a lion, and, let's face it, you don't often meet big cats strolling around the streets of our cities, Cairbre the Lion was a genuine Dub. Not only that, he was a northsider. He was born in Phoenix Park in 1919, although he wasn't allowed to roam the park preying on random deer … or cyclists. He was born in Dublin Zoo and was named after Cú Chulainn's charioteer. Maybe. Some people claimed he was called after an Irish High King. Either way, he was a very impressive pussy cat indeed, and a dude that you did not want to mess with.

He might well have happily lived out his life in Dublin Zoo, scaring the visitors by roaring at them in a genuine north Dublin accent, except that he came to the attention of another Dub. This one did not have a mane, enormous teeth or claws capable of bringing down a slow-moving gazelle. His name was Cedric Gibbons, and he was a designer who worked in the movies. Cedric, among his many other achievements in the film business, was the man who designed the golden statuette handed out as the Oscar in March every year in Hollywood. Cedric knew that one of the Hollywood studios, Metro Goldwyn Mayer (MGM), was looking for a way to spice up the company logo that appeared on screen before their films began. Why did it have to be static and boring? he thought. Why not a roaring lion? Granted, because films were silent in those days, audiences would have to imagine Cairbre's roar and would miss his Dublin accent. But he would certainly look fearsome.

In 1924, Cairbre, like many other Irish before and since, emigrated to the USA. (Actually, Dublin Zoo did a lot of business back then breeding and selling lions abroad.) Unlike most of our other emigrants, though, Cairbre made his home in Hollywood, California. MGM decided to change his name to the much-sillier-sounding Slats. Apparently, Cairbre didn't object to being called after pieces of timber, rather than (perhaps) an Irish High King or Cú Chulainn's charioteer. His career lasted until 1928 when he was replaced by another big cat called Jackie. After Jackie came Tanner, George and Leo (that last one's a bit obvious really). Cairbre/Slats went into retirement and died at the age of 17.

One last thing: you may have seen the MGM logo on TV or in the cinema (these days you actually get to hear the lion's roar), well, back in 1924 a camera crew was ordered to pop into Cairbre's cage and film their new star from inside the bars. That must have taken guts. Guts that could have ended up being snacked on by Cairbre for his lunch. You don't even want to think about how they got him to roar for the camera!

PHOTO

NAME CAIRBRE, AKA SLATS (1919-1936)

OCCUPATION(S) THOROUGHLY PROFESSIONAL LION, NORTHSIDER

MOST LIKELY TO SAY:	'C'mere to me, you' (if he could talk)
LIKES:	Meat in any form, probably including human
DISLIKES:	Movie directors and/or cameramen (unless they were tasty)
CLAIM TO FAME:	Roared (silently) before dozens of Hollywood movies in the 1920s

PADDY THE PIGEON

A courageous Irish pigeon
who brought news of D-Day, the 1944
Allied invasion of Europe.

EVEN THOUGH WHAT is now the Republic of Ireland was neutral in the Second World War (we didn't take sides), there were plenty of southern Irishmen and women involved in the most famous day of the war: D-Day, on 6 June 1944. That was when the US and British armies began to take back Europe from Nazi Germany by sending a huge force onto five beaches in Normandy, in western France.

One of our less well-known Irish D-Day heroes was a bit different to the Irish paratroopers, sailors and infantrymen. He was a pigeon named Paddy. This feathered warrior was born/hatched in Carnlough, County Antrim, and was trained as a racing pigeon by his owner, Captain Andrew Hughes, from the age of one. As Paddy was from Northern Ireland, a part of the United Kingdom, he was more likely to join the UK forces than if he had been born south of the border. And so it proved. In 1944, Paddy was recruited into the British Armed Forces and stationed at RAF Hurn in Hampshire.

Why would anyone want to conscript a pigeon? Well, because they were a reliable form of communication. Nowadays if you want to get news out from a battlefield you can send a text message (or post something on social media). Back then that wasn't a thing. The messages Paddy carried, however, were (sort of) primitive tweets! You stuck a note to his leg, and released him, and he flew home to Hampshire, where the message would be 'downloaded'.

This was done by simply removing the piece of paper, but you probably figured that out.

If a pigeon was captured by the enemy, he could be interrogated for days on end. If he finally cracked under the pressure and gave up valuable information, he became a stool pigeon (please google 'stool pigeon' – I don't want to have to explain such a really bad joke).

Paddy was one of more than 30 pigeons recruited from the British by the US Army to get coded messages back to England on D-Day. They didn't want to use radios for fear of the signal being intercepted. But the Germans were well ahead of them. They expected the use of birds as messengers, and they trained falcons with enormous talons to bring the poor pigeons down. So, not only did Paddy have to contend with bullets,

shells and strong winds, but he also had to evade the beaks and talons of German predators. Somehow he managed it, flew 368 kilometres and was the first member of the Pigeon Service to get back to Britain with the news that the Allied troops had landed successfully in Normandy.

It took him 4 hours and 50 minutes to get home. That's a phenomenal 1.27 kilometres a minute! In honour of getting bushed for the war effort, he won the animal equivalent of the famous Victoria Cross. It's called the Dickin Medal. Paddy is its only Irish winner, but that is probably because so many (southern) Irish birds and animals were expected to remain neutral in the Second World War and couldn't take part.

PHOTO

NAME PATRICK 'PADDY' THE PIGEON (1942-1954)

OCCUPATION CARRYING MESSAGES

RANK:	Are you kidding … a pigeon?
SERIAL NUMBER:	NPS 43.9451 and, yes, NPS does stand for National Pigeon Service
LIKES:	Birdseed, following winds
DISLIKES:	Bullets, shells, Nazi falcons
CLAIM TO FAME:	Only Irish winner of the Dickin Medal

GAY FUTURE

How not to make money
from a horse.

CARTMEL IS A small, remote, picturesque English town about halfway between Manchester and the Scottish border, but it is big enough to have its own racecourse. That, and its remoteness, was vitally important to an Irish betting syndicate (a group of gamblers) back in 1974, and to a horse called Gay Future.

On August Bank Holiday Monday that year, a Cork businessman named Tony Murphy put a devilish plan into action in the hope of winning half a million pounds sterling (worth about £3m today). The scam involved entering an Irish horse, called Gay Future, for a race at Cartmel. The syndicate of gamblers, led by Murphy, then placed bets on Gay Future and on two other horses who were running in races in other parts of England. With two other horses involved in the scheme, the bookies didn't realise that they stood to lose a lot of money if, for some strange reason, the other two horses didn't turn up and all the money was to go straight on to Gay Future running at Cartmel. Guess what happened? The other two horses never even left their stable yard because their trainer was in on the scheme. So, every penny of the syndicate's money was now riding on a horse whose odds were very high!

Even that didn't really raise too many alarm bells. Gay Future had been running races in Britain very unsuccessfully. He was far from being the favourite to win even a poor-quality race over the tiny Cartmel course. But that was the rub, because the Gay Future (sent over from Ireland) who actually ran the race was not the horse that had been entered and had been losing lots of races in England.

An imposter had been running as Gay Future in England while the real animal was hidden away in Ireland, ready for his big moment. There was a last-minute switch of the two horses, and it was the real Gay Future, a really fast horse, who ran at Cartmel.

By the time the bookies realised what was going on it was almost too late. Frantically, they tried to contact Cartmel to warn their colleagues to bring down the betting odds on Gay Future. This is known in racing as the 'starting price' (or SP). However, as Tony Murphy well knew, there was only one way of contacting Cartmel. That was via a telephone in a public kiosk – there were no mobile phones back then. Before Gay Future's race, Murphy made sure that one of the members of the syndicate was plonked in that phone box calling his mammy and making sure the bookies couldn't alert anyone at the course to the scam.

Gay Future won the race easily at ridiculously long odds of 10/1 (that's where you win €10 for every €1 you bet) but the bookies, having smelled a rat, refused to pay out. They called in the police and Tony Murphy ended up in court, where he was made to pay a fine for being mean to the poor bookmakers. (That's called sarcasm by the way).

PHOTO

NAME GAY FUTURE
(1970-1976)

OCCUPATION RACEHORSE

LIKES:	Grass
DISLIKES:	Bridles, whips, mean jockeys
CLAIM TO FAME:	Being used in an attempt to con a lot of English bookmakers

AFTERWORD

Thank you for getting this far.

And which one was the entirely fictional entry?

That would be Sheila McGuigan, the Irish-speaking bushranger in Australia who also had a career in law. But we don't think her *scéal* was much more ridiculous than some of the other (true) stories in the book. Irish people have done some very interesting and extraordinary things.

Pat yourself on the back if you got that right.

And thank you for not peeking (you didn't peek, right?).

ACKNOWLEDGEMENTS

To Sarah Liddy, who (unwisely) mentioned at the 2022 Irish Book Awards that if Alan and I had any other ideas for a book ... well, we couldn't resist that challenge, now could we? To Aoibheann Molumby, who then had to run with *The Forgettables* (it was called something else at first) and hack it into shape. To Mia O'Reilly for getting the word out. To Gwyneth Owen Williams, my editor of first resort, and Jonathan Williams, my wonderful agent (no relation to Gwyneth). To Nerys Williams (not related to Jonathan but Gwyneth's mother – are you still with me?) for, among many other things, introducing me to the story of Gelert and allowing me to steal it for Ireland. And to the amazing and affable (look it up) Alan Dunne, star illustrator, whom I truly do not deserve as a collaborator.

Myles

Many thanks to Sarah, Aoibheann, Mia and all at Gill Books;
your collective efforts behind the scenes have breathed life
into these pages. To Myles Dungan for yet another fantastic and
humorous insight into Irish history. To Graham Thew and Laura
Merrigan for the superb book design. To my friends and family
for their encouragement, even as they wondered where I had
disappeared to while working on this book. To my wife, Gráinne,
for all her support and to our son, Tadhg, who shares
my love of history.

Alan

THE AUTHOR

MYLES DUNGAN is a historian and broadcaster for RTÉ, currently presenting *The History Show* on RTÉ Radio I. He has written several history books for adults as well as the bestselling *Great Irish History Book* for children.

THE ILLUSTRATOR

ALAN DUNNE is an illustrator who loves making comics and picture books. He has created illustrations for museums, postage stamps, and heritage projects. In a previous life, he was a designer for RTÉ. He loves reading about history and collecting old illustrated books and newspapers, so illustrating this book was a real joy!